MW01708749

Have a Mindset to win!

Rev. Dr. Sanneth Brown

THE HOLY SPIRIT PROPHETIC POETIC DEVOTIONAL

Rev. Dr. Sanneth Brown

LifeRich
PUBLISHING®

Interior Image Credit: Latoya Brown

Scripture taken from the King James Version of the Bible.

LifeRich Publishing is a registered trademark of The Reader's Digest Association, Inc.

LifeRich Publishing books may be ordered through booksellers or by contacting:

LifeRich Publishing
1663 Liberty Drive
Bloomington, IN 47403
www.liferichpublishing.com
1 (888) 238-8637

ISBN: 978-1-4897-2346-8 (sc)
ISBN: 978-1-4897-2347-5 (hc)
ISBN: 978-1-4897-2345-1 (e)

Library of Congress Control Number: 2019908338

Print information available on the last page.

LifeRich Publishing rev. date: 07/10/2019

I will praise thee; for I am fearfully and wonderfully made: marvellous are thy works; and that my soul knoweth right well. (Psalm 139:14)

But thou, O Lord, art a shield for me; my glory, and the lifter up of mine head. (Psalm 3:3)

And Jabez called on the God of Israel, saying, Oh that thou wouldest bless me indeed, and enlarge my coast, and that thine hand might be with me, and that thou wouldest keep me from evil, that it may not grieve me! And God granted him that which he requested. (1 Chronicles 4:10)

Hear my cry, O God; attend unto my prayer. From the end of the earth will I cry unto thee, when my heart is overwhelmed: lead me to the rock that is higher than I. For thou hast been a shelter for me, and a strong tower from the enemy. (Psalm 61:1–3)

Dedication

First, I dedicate this Devotional book to the Trinity, God the Father, the Son, and the Holy Ghost. I am eternally indebted to You, God, for everything You have done in my life. You brought me a mighty long way and is still the keeper of my life. You've always believed in me. You are the most important part of my life story. You give me a reason to smile. You brighten my world. You transformed my life and made it brand new. Your love for me shines brighter in my heart than the sun, the moon, and the stars. God, You are my all in all. You are my deliverer, healer, provider, protector, defender, confidant, advocate, comforter, best friend, and the bishop of my soul!

Second, I would like to dedicate this Devotional book to Albert Edwards, my oldest brother and the first of fourteen children, and to Evadney Walker, my oldest sister and the third of fourteen children. Thanks a million to both of you for paving the way for my family and me to come to Canada—a resourceful, peaceful and beautiful country—so that I could pursue my dreams, visions, and revelations. It would not have been possible for me to achieve all that I have and will in the future if it weren't for you both. You were both the hands and feet of God. You both answered the call to bring your mother, father, and five siblings to Canada. I rise to call you both blessed, resilient, resolute, adaptable, ambitious, considerate, adventurous, strong, capable, amiable, magnificent, sympathetic, understanding, and impartial. I love and respect you both. I will cherish your phenomenal help in my heart forever. You are both loved, adored, cherished, and appreciated. May the God of Abraham, Isaac, and Jacob bless and cover you all the days of your lives. I am praying steadfastly for you both. I give thumbs-up to my big brother and big sister.

Third, I would like to dedicate this Devotional book to Rev. Minitha

Brown-Thomas, Rev. Patricia Bryan, Rev. Carla Wallen, Rev. Valerie Bryan, Rev. Latoya Brown, Minister Chelsey Clarke, and Leslie Clarke. You all have stood by me in ministry in such a way that heaven will surely be your reward. Your faithful labor of love will never be forgotten. Your steadfastness, dedication, and commitment while standing with me will always be remembered. In good times and bad, you all were there supporting me. When others turned their backs on me, when betrayal cut deep, and when disappointments kept knocking at my door, your determined, smiling faces, prayers, and encouragements gave me great hope to carry on with the gospel of Jesus Christ. You have been an enormous source of strength, hope, comfort, and courage in my life and ministry. In my sorrows, you all were my rock. You are all reapers of generational legacies of greatness, blessings, unstoppable favors, goodness, prosperity, wealth, success, and so much more. I had to press through some dark times, but your relentless inspiration, powerful motivational prayers, and words kept me pushing ahead, knowing that one day, I would see God's mighty promises come to pass. Thanks a million for never giving up on me. I love, cherish, adore, and appreciate all of you. Thanks for having my back. I love you all endlessly.

Fourth, I also dedicate this Devotional to my handsome, God-blessed, Christ-centered, chosen, anointed, and appointed son and Author, Rev. Darron Bailey Jr. You are, indeed the apple of God's eye. The fruit of my womb is blessed forever and ever. You are the pride and joy of my life. You are my gifted Prophet Samuel and Jeremiah, who declared and decreed prophetic precise and accurate utterances in season and out. You have encouraged me in ways that I cannot find words to articulate. Know that you have a heart of gold. You are indeed God's deep, divine mouthpiece, who is destined for greatness. You are the reaper of generational legacies of greatness, blessings, unstoppable favors, goodness, prosperity, wealth, success, and so much more. Don't let anyone or anything stop you from catapulting to the third heaven and beyond. Huge celebratory generational blessings are awaiting you in this life and the life to come. Stand fast in the liberty of Jesus Christ. Keep the entire armour of God on at all times to defeat the enemy's traps. I love you from earth to heaven. You are irreplaceable.

Fifth, I dedicate this Devotional book to all readers who desire a higher level of intimacy with Christ Jesus and a deeper dimension of the Holy Ghost.

Contents

Dedication vii
Preface xi
Acknowledgments xiii

Chapter 1 Words Are Powerful, So Watch Your Words 1
Chapter 2 There Is No God Like You, Jehovah 4
Chapter 3 I Come to the High Courts of Heaven with My Petitions 7
Chapter 4 You Are Standing Upon the Rock, but Your Faith Is Still Wavering 14
Chapter 5 You Shall Leap over Walls and Run through the Enemy's Troops 17
Chapter 6 Pressing through Frustration 21
Chapter 7 The "I Will" Promises of God in the Bible 25
Chapter 8 Rise above Your Circumstances 30
Chapter 9 When Feelings of Unworthiness Come to You, Tell Yourself that You Are Worthy 33
Chapter 10 It's Extremely Important to Assess the People Who Come into Your Life 36
Chapter 11 Guard-Your-Ears Gate 41
Chapter 12 Heaven Holds the Secret for Your Life: Pain, Heartbreak, Hurt, and Disappointments 48
Chapter 13 When You Stay in the Secret Place, Visions Are Made Clear 53
Chapter 14 When the Creator Made You, He Put No Limits on You 59
Chapter 15 The Awesomeness of God Will Deliver You 64

Chapter 16 An Eternal Fire of Worship Has Risen in the Hearts of God's People.......... 68
Chapter 17 Jesus Christ Is the Friend of All Friends.......... 73
Chapter 18 Guard-Your Eyes Gate.......... 79
Chapter 19 Lord, May You Smell the Sweet Aroma of My Praise and Worship.......... 85
Chapter 20 Having Sweet Peace Within.......... 90
Chapter 21 Walking the Narrow Road Is Not an Easy Journey.......... 96
Chapter 22 The Acronym of Power and Courage.......... 100
Chapter 23 Let Your Life Speak for You.......... 104
Chapter 24 I Am Wrapped up in Jesus Christ.......... 108
Chapter 25 Stay in the Race.......... 113

About the Author.......... 119

Preface

This Devotional book is designed to empower your body, soul, mind, and spirit. It will uplift you to a higher level in Jesus Christ daily. It will help you get closer to God. It will advance you into unknown spiritual territories and new dimensions that you have never been to before.

This Devotional book will help you freshly approach the Bible. You will see things infinitely and not finitely. You will understand the truths of the Bible more genuinely. You will learn how to apply the word of God effectively to your life in a personal way. This Devotional book will boost your self-image/self-esteem. This Devotional book will draw you into the depths of the Spirit. The supernatural power in you will definitely come forth stronger than ever. This Devotional book is rooted in scriptures that can help you unpack the Word of God through pictures. It is a life-transforming book!

Acknowledgments

Thanks a million to The New Testament Church of Christ The Redeemer of Canada's members for their amazing, outstanding, and courageous prayers, fasting, love, prophetic precise, accurate utterances, kindness, generosity, and continued support. All of you desire the best for me. All of you constantly encourage me to catapult to the third heaven. I will never forget all of you. You all gave me the courage to go forward and fight the good fight of faith. Your continued support means the world to me. You all care and love me in exceptional ways. Words are never enough to express my sincere and heartfelt gratitude. I appreciate, love, and cherish you all. I love you all from the bottom of my heart. You are all God's determined eagles soaring to the next dimension in the Holy Ghost. Heaven blesses you all. Thanks for standing with me and believing God for me. Thanks a million for who you all are; mighty men and women of valour! I declare and decree the covenant and blessings of Abraham, Isaac, and Jacob are upon you all now and forever, amen.

To all my family, Thanks a million for your continued support, love, goodness, encouragements, commitment, and faithfulness. You are all blessed to be a blessing. You are all God's chosen generation destined for greatness. You are all set apart and called by God to do great exploits on the earth. I declare and decree God's richest blessings upon you all!

Thanks a million to Calvin Brown and Pauline Brown: You are both amazing, caring, loving, peaceful, unstoppable, decisive, versatile, fearless, and ambitious. Thanks for looking out for me. I will never forget both of you powerful words of encouragements, motivation, and inspiration that has strengthened me to move forward in life. The covenant and blessings of Abraham, Isaac, and Jacob are upon you both always and forever.

Thanks to my delightful older brother and loving sister in law. You are both champions of love and hope!

Kamoy Bartley, sincere thanks for your continued support, encouragements, kindness, goodness, heartfelt love, and sincerity. You are God's masterpiece. You are chosen, anointed, and blessed to be a blessing. You are loving, courageous, amicable, and empathetic. God's surely goodness and mercy are following you all the days of your life. God is propelling you deeper into the supernatural realm. You are God's chosen remnant!

Mother Vida Hosey, thanks a million for your prayers, encouragements, love, kindness, goodness, and continued support. You are God's chosen vessel. You are ninety-three years old. You possess a wealth of knowledge. Your Bible reading and knowledge is incredible. May God strengthen, keep, and bless you all the days of your life. May His peace, joy, and blessings rest upon you daily. You are smart, courageous, beautiful, beloved, blissful, and determine. You are loved, cherished, and appreciated.

Pastor Vanessa Wheatle, thanks a million for your sincere love, goodness, kindness, prayers, fasting, encouragements, scriptures, commitment, loyalty, and faithfulness. You are anointed and appointed to sing, preach, and teach God's potent word. Your voice is amazing. You are God's champion of hope soaring to unfathomable heights. God is with you. Fear not He will uphold you with the righteousness of His right hand — Deborah's anointing is on your life. You are a victorious winner!

Minister Tesharah Briscoe, Humungous thanks for all your support, goodness, kindness, love, commitment and sincerity. It is never overlooked. You are God's anointed singer. Your songs always blessed my heart. May God increase you more and more each day. May His peace, grace, joy, happiness, and victory surrounds you always. Deborah's anointing is on your life, so continue to soar greater than the eagles. You are God's unstoppable warrior!

Shernet Dryden, thanks a million for your continued prayers, fasting, support, faithfulness, commitment, encouragements, love, weekly scriptures, and prophetic precise and accurate utterances are always appreciated. You are God's masterpiece, who has been created in His image to do great exploits in this world. May God continue to bless, keep, and strengthen you. Continue to soar to heights unknown. You are God's unstoppable stalwart.

Fabian Livingston and Stacey-Ann Lewis, thanks a million for your prayers, fasting, scriptures, encouragements, goodness, love and continued support. Your words and advice to me are always sound. God is your everlasting portion. Continue to dwell in the secret place of the Most High God. I declare and decree that the great plans of God over your lives will come to fruition. May the anointing of God fall afresh on you both daily. You are both smart, courageous, creative, adventitious, ambitious, amiable, and resolute. May you both experience His glory and power in a new way this season. The best is yet to come. You are both God's victorious stalwarts. You are both winners!

Pastor Calmeta Page, my heart is full of gratitude for your constant prayers, encouragements, kindness, goodness, love, scriptures, and continued support. Your words are powerful and true. You are God's chosen warrior. You are going deeper and deeper in God, and you will discover the great plans He has in store for you. You are God's anointed stalwart.

Evangelist Adelenia Wellington, Humungous thanks for your relentless prayers, fasting, encouragements, scriptures, goodness, love, and prophetic, precise, accurate, divine utterances. Your daily encouraging words are life-changing. Your love for God is real and tangible. Your hope in God is steadfast. You are God's anointed, appointed and chosen warrior, great intercessor, and shinning sunbeam. You are bold, courageous, amicable, diligent, and faithful. You are loved, cherished, and appreciated. Deborah's anointing is on your life. Go forth and possess the land in Jesus's mighty name. Continue to dance your way to victory!

To all my friends that are bishops, prophets, apostles, missionaries, pastors, evangelists, and teachers, thanks very much for your prayers, fasting, love, goodness, encouragements, scriptures, precise and accurate prophetic utterances from the Holy Ghost, and continued support. God is your restorer and deliverer. He is your on-time God. Shine on with His glory.

Everton Edmondson, Thanks very much for your relentless prayers, fasting, love, goodness, encouragements, and precise and accurate prophetic utterances. You are God's anointed stalwart. Continue to manifest the glory of God. God is with you never to leave you alone. Favor is upon you. He will calm ever storm that you face. Your many lifelines are always divine and appreciated. You are anointed to preach and teach the infallible word of God.

Andrea Pitter, thanks a million for your ongoing prayers, fasting, encouragements, love, goodness, faithfulness, commitment, loyalty, and continued support. You are God's anointed, amazing singer with a voice that can transform lives. The world awaits your CDs. You are a courageous, ambitious, amusing, communicative, smart, diligent, determined, chosen warrior. The Davidic covenant and blessings are upon you. You are a true, dynamic worshipper. Worship eagle shine on. You are unstoppable.

Minister Kathleen Baisden, Gigantic Thanks for all your prayers, fasting, goodness, kindness, encouragements, scriptures, and continued support. Your help in ministry will always be remembered. You are God's anointed teacher and preacher of the gospel of Jesus Christ. God is your steadfast rock and sure foundation. May the God of heaven grant you peace, comfort, restoration, and victory. You are God's worship warrior with an amazing voice that the world needs to hear and be set free. You are courageous, creative, and bold.

Paula Thomas, thanks a million for all your sincere love, goodness, kindness, commitment, faithfulness, prayers, encouragements, and continued support. You are a dynamic, courageous, resourceful, communicable, intelligent, creative, and skilled Citysites Realty-Salesperson for over fifteen years. I declare and decree that everything that you put your hands to do will prosper in the mighty name of Jesus. You are destined for God's best, and nothing less will you settle for. You are on the winning side of life. You are victorious.

Bishop Donald Lowe and Evangelist Marlene Lowe, Thanks a million to both of you for your relentless prayers, fasting, encouragements, precise and accurate Holy Ghost prophetic utterances, love, goodness, kindness, and powerful scriptures. You are both God's chosen remnants set-apart to bring Him glory for such a time as this. You are not forgotten. May the God of all peace and comfort fill your hearts daily and perfect all your hearts desires in Him. God is your solid foundation. Hold fast to God's strong hands. The Cyrus anointing is on you both.

Pastor Vendetta Anderson-Mctaggart and Co-Pastor Courtney

Mctaggart, thanks sincerely from the bottom of my heart to both of you for your love, goodness, prayers, encouragements, scriptures, prophetic precise and accurate utterances and continued support. You are both soaring to unfathomable heights in the power of the Holy Ghost. You are both blessed to be a blessing. The hands of God is heavily upon you both. Continue to run the race that is ahead of you.

Minister Sophia Buchanan, heartfelt thanks for your weekly prayers, fasting, scriptures, encouragements, dedication, faithfulness, and support. You are God's chosen diadem. The Davidic covenant and blessings are upon you. You are God's chosen warrior like King David was. You are strong, bold, creative, and courageous. You are God's anointed, true worshiper.

Dr. Michael Reid and Pastor Yvette Reid, thanks a million for all your prayers, fasting, prophetic precise, accurate utterances, love, encouragements, goodness, and continued support. Both of you are God's anointed, appointed and set apart remnants for such a time as this. You are both appreciated. You are both destined for God's greatness. You are two determined mighty eagles soaring to unfathomable heights. Both of you will never be forgotten. The Breaker's anointing is on you both. Continue to run the race that is before you both. Your rewards will be great!

To Marcia Walker at Styles Unisex Hair Salon and Barbers Shop, thanks a million for being my hairstylist for over twenty years. You are naturally talented, gifted, creative, brilliant, bold, brave, and courageous. God is your refuge and strength. May you always rise above all the plans of the enemy. You are loving, kindhearted, generous, giving, caring, unique, innovative, adaptable, and genuine. May God bless all your endeavors.

Patrice Williams and Janet Gordon, Gigantic thanks for your love, goodness, kindness, prayers, encouragements, and support. You are both amazing, courageous, bold, brave, creative, and ambitious. You are both God's precious jewels. You both have greatness within. You are both God's unstoppable force to be reckoned with.

Amberlyn DeNobrega, thanks a million for your ongoing support, goodness, kindness, prayers, encouragements, scriptures, and steadfast love. You are God's precious jewel and empowered gem. Explore all that God has in store for you. His plans for you are great. He desires to prosper you. Queen Esther's favour is definitely upon you. You are intelligent, beautiful, adventitious, creative, enthusiastic, fearless, and gregarious. Bring out the greatness that is within you. You were born to win!

Darren Winston, deep heartfelt thanks for your goodness, kindness, continued support, encouragements, and the desire to advance the kingdom of God. It is highly regarded. You are God's awesome masterpiece. His plans for you are great. May God's divine peace, joy, and grace rest upon you always. May God overflow you with His goodness and mercy.

Valora Bryan, thanks a million for your ongoing prayers, fasting, love, goodness, hospitality, caring and sharing ways. Thanks for the many times that you have hosted me while I was on a mission for the Lord. You are God's amazing, tenacious, beautiful, brave, blessed, bold, and courageous stalwart. May God extend your territories and borders. May you continue to see the goodness of the Lord in the land of the living. May the blessings of the Lord rest upon you always.

Rev. Grace Smith, sincere thanks to you for your awesome support in ministry. Your labor is not in vain. Thanks for your countless prayers, fasting, encouragements, kindness, graciousness, faithfulness, commitment, and dedication. You are creative, talented, and courageous. Your effort is appreciated. You are indeed anointed to preach and teach the potent word of God. May God spread your wings so you can fly. Be strong in the Lord and in the power of His might.

Naseer Asghary of Bride's Night Wedding Photography, thanks a million, for taking such beautiful, radiant pictures for me and permitting me to use them in my books. Thanks for your continued support, commitment, and faithfulness. May God prosper and bless all your endeavors. You are a born winner!

Late Evangelist Shirley Francis, you may be gone but, you will never be forgotten. Your sweet memories still live on in my heart forever. I am truly grateful for your many prayers, fasting, love, goodness, powerfully divine encouragements, and scriptures. You always inspired and motivated me to continue to carry the cross of Jesus Christ throughout this world to the lost and dying. Your positive words stuck fast to my soul and enlightened my spirit. Your dancing was electric and contagious. I love you all the time. I sure miss your old-fashioned gospel singing. You are gone but will always remain in my heart. You were God's anointed singer and worshiper.

Missionary Linda Edwards, thanks a million for being my amazing hairdresser for twenty years. Thanks for your love, goodness, kindness, courage, prayers, scriptures, encouragements, commitment, dedication, and faithfulness. You could have given up on me, but you chose to hold the fort and fight the good fight of faith. You are loved, cherished, and appreciated. Thanks for having my back for many years and standing with me wholeheartedly. May God richly bless you. You are blessed to be a blessing.

To Evangelist Carmetta Clarke, thanks a million for your endless love, prayers, fasting, encouragements, scriptures, goodness, love, gracefulness, commitment, faithfulness, loyalty, and continued support. You are a tower of strength to me, and I will always remember you. You are God's determined eagle soaring to the next dimension. You are loved, cherished, and appreciated. You are an unstoppable stalwart for Jehovah. God will reward you greatly in due season.

Marsha Fagan, Humongous thanks for your sincere love, goodness, prayers, encouragements, and continued support. You are indeed chosen to declare the unadulterated gospel of Jesus Christ. God is on your side. His goodness and mercy will always follow you. You are destined to win. You are blessed to be a blessing. You are courageous, bold, and successful.

Minister Ruschelle Buchanan, thanks a great deal, for your prayers, fasting, scriptures, kindness, goodness, encouragements and wonderful support in ministry. It is appreciated and will not go unnoticed. I will always be grateful for the time spent in the ministry. You are God's champion destined for greatness. May the power of the Holy Ghost arise within you and soar with you beyond the veil. You are anointed and appointed to preach and teach God's relevant word. You are courageous, creative, bold, hospitable, and innovative. May God's blessings be upon you always!

Pastor Marvia Providence, sincere heartfelt gratitude for all your love, prayers, fasting, encouragements, prophetic precise, accurate utterances, kindness, goodness, and continued support. Arise and shine for the glory of the Lord is risen upon you. It's your season of great advancements worldwide. Your goals are achievable. God has no limits on you. You are an anointed stalwart. Your voice is remarkable, and it has transformed many lives.

Debbie Samuel, thanks very much for all your love, prayers,

encouragements, scriptures, weekly quotes, and support. May the blessing of the Lord be upon you that makes rich and adds no sorrow. You are an anointed, true worshiper.

Pastor Roasalee Diles, thanks a million for being you—sincere, loving, caring, sharing, genuine, good, kind, giving, courageous, ambitious, and successful. I will always cherish your daily prayers, social media encouragements, scriptures, and on-time, precise, and accurate Holy Ghost utterances. The favor of God is upon you forever. You are a determined eagle soaring to new heights. You are an agent of change in my life. You deserve God's best. You are God's devoted champion. You were born to win!

To Rev. Valerie Bryan, Dr. Audrey Shepherd, Pastor Nadine Brown-Fuller, Pastor Rudolph Flemmings, Evangelist Jennifer Flemmings, Minister Nicola Thompson, Evangelist Lillian Allison, Minister Carolyn Smart, Minister Shameika Hue, Dr. Patricia Keith, Minister Robin Keith, Rev. Dorothy Richards, Pastor Alma Aiken, Minister Sharon Smith-Wheatle, Minister Bernice Wiltshire, Evangelist Veronica Morgan, Evangelist Theresa Wright, Minister Trevaughan Baisden-Smith, Minister Tavaughan Baisden-Smith, Minister Kyle Thompson, Rev. Venese DeNobrega, Rev. Minitha Brown-Thomas, Rev. Patricia Bryan, Minister Marva Stewart-Black, Rev. Brian Robinson, Rev. Leopold Livingston, Lay Pastor Everton Wheatle, and Author Rev. Darron Bailey Jr: Thanks a million for being such great intercessors for me. You have all spent time daily in deep intercessory prayers and fastings for me against the many relentless attacks that I face from my adversaries. I don't have enough words to articulate the way I feel deep inside me. I truly cherish and appreciate all your sincere intercessory prayers to see me advance in the kingdom of God and for my personal life. Heaven blesses you all. May God, reward you all greatly. Intercessors are needed today more than ever. Continue to stand in the gap for God's chosen leaders and His people. God is calling willing and available intercessors that will be selfless and will cry out for the nations. You are all on the right path. Your daily sound words of divine depth, confirmation, and affirmation are always appreciated. All of you give me great hope to fight on to victory instead of giving up. You are God's anointed conduits.

Redeemer Oil of Joy team and weekly intercessors (Pastor Tanya

Mclean, Minister Roy Dart, Missionary Barbara Bodnar, Rev. Adia Douglas, Evangelist Yvonne Bell, Missionary Shennet Bryan, Minister Osalita Williams, Evangelist Shawniel Vassell, Sheldon Vassell, Minister Kathleen Elliott, Minister Karen Thompson, Minister Pauline Fuller, Minister Luicilda Bleary, Rev. Karen Proudlove-Brown, Minister Valerie Rodney, Patricia Foster, Rev. Shawnita Donaldson, Evangelist Phillippa Stewart, Evangelist Ruby Smith, Rev. Carla Wallen, Rev. Paula Roach, Rev. Mildred Ellis, Rev. Karen Grant, Minister Mellecia Jones-Livingston, Evangelist Sophia Brown- Robinson, Minister Charles Brown, Minister Nadine Justus, Missionary Ina Hechavarria, Evangelist Walda Brown, Missionary Cathleen Campbell, Minister Sabrena Dayle, Opal Dayle, Patricia Douglas, Pastor Valerie Mitchell, Rev. Latoya Brown, Rev. Shermane Watkin, and Evangelist Marlett Brown): Thanks a million to all of you for your unwavering continued support, weekly intercessory prayers, fastings, faithfulness, commitment, loyalty, on-time, precise, and accurate Holy Ghost prophetic utterances, steadfast love, dedication, and devotion. All of you are never afraid to express to me what God has laid on your hearts. You're weekly encouragements through voice messages, texts, emails, and on social media is imprinted on my heart forever. Continue to soar to the third heaven. I am forever grateful. You are all doing a great job. Don't come down. May God catapult you to heights that exceed your expectations. May the God of grace, peace, comfort, healing, and joy fill your hearts. May the blessings of the Lord rest on you all. May He bless all your endeavors. All of you are victorious.

Redeemer's amazing Children and Youth, thanks a million for all your love and continued sincere support. You are all extremely creative, beautiful, marvelous, ambitious, intellectual, intuitive, inventive, and energetic. You are all superstars in my eyes. You have encouraged me with your kind words, gestures, pictures of myself that make me laugh out loud, cards, phone calls, love, care, compassion, goodness, prayers, and constant smiles. You make me joyful while serving the Lord. You are all destined for God's greatness. All of you are born to win and to be wise.

Elliott Lewis, Kishon Thompson, Ezekiel Wallen, Raheem Proudlove, Raheem Proudlove, Nathanael Williams, Shemar Graham, Akeem Bowley, Rhaheem Bowley, Trevon Thomas, Jalan G, Michael G, Joshua G, John H, Alex P, Ismael B, Isaac W, Le-Sonn P, Alijah B, Kayden B, Marcus

B, Joshua B, David W, Joseph W, Isaac B, Josiah C, Noah D, Trustin D, Caleb S-W, Gabriel L, Jeremiah R, Elijah T, Terrence B, Treyvon B, and Jeremiah L: Thanks a bunch for your heartfelt words of hope, comfort, joy, kindness, and goodness. You are all great champions for God. You are a generation that is as bold as a lion. You are all courageous, unstoppable, fearless, intelligent, persistent, and philosophical. God is fighting for you all, so you are all winners.

Chauntel Thomas, Thea Baisden, Tiana Brown, Abigail Williams, Quiana Smith-Wheatle, Keishauna Smith-Wheatle, Kriston Brown, Jordyn D, Patina Bryan, DreAnn Dyer, Tenae Brown, Aliyah Patrick, Aaliyah D, Reanne G, Angelene C, Ava D, Abigail B, Tameka Brown, Danique S, Stephanie M, Saniya B, Sierra B, Storm S, Chaya B, Aliza B, Jaeden G, Sarah B, Zoey P, Tiana C, Sarah S, Chanecia H, Hannah R, Naomi T, and Adelina P: Heartfelt gratitude to all of you, for your singing, dancing, praising, worshiping, and amazing participation in the ministry. You are all God's precious jewels moving forward to unfathomable heights. All of you are fearfully, wonderfully, and uniquely created by God. God did not put any limits on you all. You are all intelligent, creative, diligent, vibrant, powerful, sensible, gregarious, courageous, and sincere. You have all touched my life in numerous ways. You all put a smile on my face every week. The amazing things you all said to me makes me laugh out loud. You are all extraordinary sunbeams!

Josanne Garraway, thanks a million for your love, goodness, prayers, encouragements, scriptures and continued support. You are called for such a time as this to shine your light in this dark world, for others to see and come along. Queen Esther's favour is upon you. You are blessed to be a blessing. You are courageous, unstoppable, ambitious, inventive, and intelligent. Don't give up; the best is yet to come.

Ian Graham and Andrew Peart, thanks a great deal for all your prayers, goodness, commitment, faithfulness, loyalty, and continued support. It means a lot to me knowing that you both want to see the kingdom of God advance for His glory. May the blessings of the Lord rest upon you both always and forever. You are both mighty men of valour!

A million thanks to Minister McLaren Alphonso for all your prayers, fasting, goodness, kindness, faithfulness, commitment, loyalty, and continued support. Heaven is your limit. You are God's rare gem and worship warrior. I appreciate, love, and cherish you always. You labor relentlessly and willingly in the ministry. You are an exceptional, versatile, creative, anointed musician. May God bless you, richly. The Davidic covenant and blessings are upon you.

Thanks a million to Pastor Jacqueline Stubbs for your invaluable contribution, prayers, fasting, goodness, love, faithfulness, encouragements, commitment, loyalty, and continued support. Your prophetic precise, accurate utterances will never go unnoticed. Your labor is not in vain. God orders your steps. I declare that God will bless you and reward you richly. You are God's brave stalwart. You are a dynamic, intelligent remnant soaring to unfathomable heights in the Holy Ghost. You are a great source of strength to me. God's richest blessings are upon you. You are anointed to preach and teach the infallible word of God. Go forth In God's might and power.

Thanks a million to my three dearest and beloved friends, Rev. Faurel Davis, Murine Blake, and Judith Barnaby for your unfailing love, courage, prayers, fasting, kindness, goodness, generosity, faithfulness, loyalty, and continued support. Your friendship is cordial, affable, lasting, and beneficial. Your motives are genuine. All of you have my best interests at heart, and for that, I am super grateful. You are all so helpful and kind. You are all beautiful, inside and out. You all inspire and motivated me and bring out the best in me. Nothing can stop you all. You are all making a bigger impact than you realize. Continue to grow in God. I love, cherish, and appreciate our friendship for over thirty-three years and counting — the covenant and blessings of Abraham, Isaac, and Jacob are all yours in Jesus's mighty name. You are all champions of hope and love. There are no limits to what God will do in your lives. Love you all now and forever. Bravo!

Rev. Shermane Watkin, thanks a million for your sincere, unwavering, continued support through your daily prayers, fasting, love, kindness, goodness, steadfast service, dedication, and faithfulness. You could have walked away, but your love for the ministry and me remained untouched. For such, I am very grateful. Twelve years and counting is proof of the sincere heart you have to see me advance, and the kingdom of God extends to greater territories. You are God's anointed, appointed, warrior of praise, worship, and music. Indeed, I call you God's prayer eagle. Victory is yours in Jesus's mighty name. There is no limit to where God will take you. You are blessed beyond measure.

Rev. Valerie Bryan, thanks a million for your generosity, love, care, kindness, goodness, friendship, prayers, faithfulness, generosity, dedication, on-time, precise, and accurate prophetic utterances, encouragements, and weekly scriptures. Your labor is not in vain. Thanks for your countless intercessory prayers and fasting for this project. Continue to reach heights in the supernatural realm. God's favor, blessings, and restoration are upon you. Deborah's anointing is upon you. You have been anointed and appointed to declare the potent word of God for His glory. You are a treasured asset in the kingdom of God. You are blessed to be a blessing.

Minister Chelsey Clarke and Leslie Clarke, thanks a million for all your continued and unwavering support, love, goodness, kindness, faithfulness, commitment, dedication, creativity, and loyalty. You are both God's unstoppable warriors and chosen vessels that will bring forth His glory on the earth. Soar to unknown heights in this season. May unexpected favors locate you both. Your talents and gifts will make room for both of you. God will extend your territories and borders.

Rev. Patricia Bryan, thanks a million for your relentless, unstoppable, and continued support in ways that words cannot describe. Thanks for being a great, sincere, loving, kindhearted, encourager, uplifting giver of precise and accurate Holy Ghost utterances that always come right on time. Words fail to express my love for you but know this; you are an inspiration and motivation in my life. You give me reasons to go on when quitting looks easier. I am deeply touched by and admire your class, elegance, and attention to details. You are reliable, generous, kindhearted, friendly, adaptable, dependable, accountable, and approachable. You possess great leadership characteristics. You are amazingly creative in all that you do. Your love for me is genuine. Our connection is root deep, and I will not let anything or anyone separate us. God has great plans for your life. Thanks for praying this project to fruition. You are the apple of God's eye and a real warrior for God. Shine on to victory. The Davidic covenant and blessings are upon you. I love you forever.

Rev. Carla Wallen, thanks a million for always looking out for me. You love and care about me in ways I will always remember. Thank you for your countless encouragements, on-time, precise, and accurate Holy

Ghost utterances, love, courage, hope, goodness, kindness, hospitality, and continued support in my life and ministry. You are indeed God's stalwart, chosen gem, spirit-filled gospel preacher, singer, warrior, and so much more. You are ambitious, courageous, creative, faithful, tenacious, dedicated, beautiful, and intelligent. The world awaits your CDs. You are a determined eagle soaring to a new level in God. I will love you always. You are anointed to preach and teach the unadulterated gospel of Jesus Christ. You are unstoppable.

Rev. Latoya Brown, thanks a million for your amazing support of this Devotional book. Thanks for the artwork for my book and the permission to use them commercially. I sincerely appreciate you. You are talented, creative, and gifted. Continue to soar to unknown heights with your talents. You are destined for greatness. Let the God-given gifts, that are inside you, come forth. You are God's anointed vessel. Favor is on the horizon for you. You are indeed courageous, bold, faithful, dedicated, brilliant, intelligent, anointed, appointed, and called out to be the difference. You are loved, cherished, and appreciated. I love you always.

Rev. Louise Gordon, Evangelist Grace Brown, and Rev. Vernal Brown, thanks a million for declaring loud and clear that all of you are not ashamed of the gospel of Jesus Christ. It's uplifting to know that my big sisters and older brother are serving the Lord. May God grant you all the strength and anointing to run this gospel race wholeheartedly and as His great stalwarts. Know that your little sister is watching you all live for Jesus Christ. It's a joy to know that our late mother and father are proud of all of us. All of you have strengthened me by your continued love, fasting, prayers, encouragements, scriptures, and anointed on-time, precise, and accurate Holy Ghost utterances. I declare that generational blessings will fall upon all of you daily. You are all blessed to be a blessing. May the blessings of God be your portion. Love you all forever.

Rev. Minitha Brown-Thomas, thanks a million for your relentless prayers, fasting, love, daily scriptures, and encouragements. Your prophetic, on-time, precise, and accurate Holy Ghost utterances always come at the time when I need them most. My big sister, thanks also for standing with me in the ministry. You could have run, but you chose to stay the course. I am deeply grateful for your love and care towards me from childhood to adulthood. You always provided for me when I was a child and even now. I still cherish those unforgettable moments when you came through for me. You are, no doubt, a hardworking, ambitious, tenacious, talented, creative, courageous, Christ-centered, adventurous, prosperous, successful, bold, and brave woman of might and power. You are the perfect example of a real overcomer and still, stand in spite of the many problems Satan throws at you. You rise above all your problems. You are resilient. Jesus is your divine and ultimate source. God is your refuge and strength. He is your rock of ages. Jesus is the pillar that supports your life. Thanks for making this project possible. May the blessings of God continue to rest upon you. Thanks for having my back at all times. My love for you is solid.

Author, Rev. Darron Bailey Jr, thanks a billion for all that you are to me and then some. You are my strength when I am very weak. You are my goodness in times of darkness. You put a loud hallelujah inside my heart even when I am feeling low. You are loved, cherished, adored, and appreciated. You take personal growth very seriously. You are passionate about God and the things of His kingdom. I love your enthusiasm for life. You have a big heart for children and youth. You have the greatest imagination. You are very loving, caring, tenacious, sincere, Christ-centered, adventurous, chosen, anointed, appointed, gifted, and blessed. You are an amazing, outstanding, and wonderful son to me. I would never exchange you for anyone else. You will be catapulted to the third heaven. Your laughter is contagious. You give me reasons to smile even in difficult times. I am eternally grateful for your endless prayers, fasting, and daily intercession for me. Thanks for your courageous support in seeing that this project would be fulfilled as God spoke it long ago. Thanks for believing and embracing my many dreams, visions, and revelations. You bring out the utmost best in me. For that, I am so grateful. Continue to be a role model, a great inspiration, and a motivator for today's children and youth. May you move from glory to glory, victory to victory, from grace to grace, from level to level, and from anointing to anointing. Heaven is your limit!

Chapter 1

Words Are Powerful, So Watch Your Words

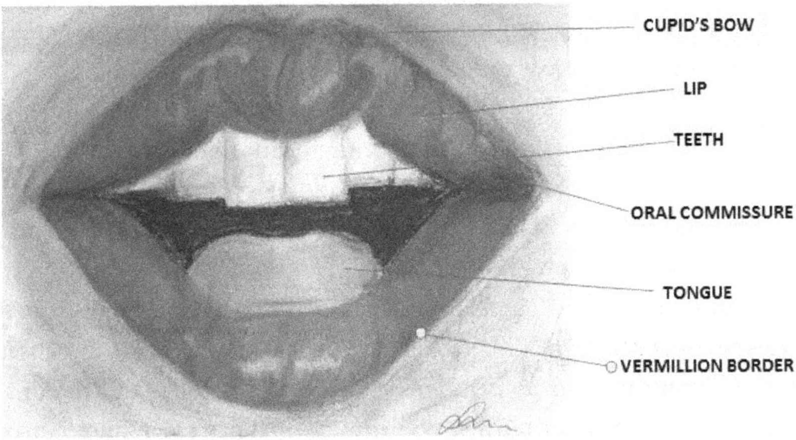

> Death and life are in the power of the tongue: and they that love it shall eat the fruit thereof. (Proverbs 18:21)

Words give life to some and death to others. Your words can kill and heal. Your words can mend and scatter. They can come to the forefront of your heart in peace or destroy your heart and cause bitterness. You should speak words of hope to others, and in return, they should speak words of hope to you. Positive words give life a greater meaning.

Words are transforming and radiating to the soul, body, mind, and spirit. Positive words can be used to calm an atmosphere. Positive words can give so much power to a dead soul bringing forth a resurrected life.

Words can give a new beginning to a hopeless life. Words can cause the rebirth of one's destiny, calling, and ministry.

When negative words are spoken to an already depressed mind, it can push a person to the edge of suicide. Negative words that are spoken over children can cause them to have negative, defeating behaviors throughout their life span if they are not reversed. It's important to speak life over your children. It's important to speak words of hope, peace, love, joy, goodness, and kindness over your children daily. Positive words give people a sense of worth and an excellent chance of surviving this brutal world.

Words are not to be used carelessly but should be given much thought before they leave the mouth. At one point, we all have spoken words we have regretted. We cannot take these words back. They hurt others and sometimes damage good relationships. All humans can honestly admit to doing this, whether it was intentional or not. No one is perfect; therefore, human beings are subject to follies. We all have faults within us.

It's good to be honest with ourselves so that healing can begin. Let's speak truth to ourselves and let the healing begin right now.

When I was a child, I spake as a child, I understood as a child, I thought as a child: but when I became a man, I put away childish things. (1 Corinthians 13:11)

Words cut deeper than sharp razors do. They slice through us better than they slice through tomatoes. They eat at us more than some disease does. They torment us as hell does. They scatter people and nations as horrible winds do. They burn as wildfires burn. They creep into our souls and cause decay. They lurk in our bodies and cause us to degenerate. They enter our bodies and fully infect us.

Speak words that strengthen others. Speak words that are empowering and praiseworthy. Speak words that uplift others. Speak words that are bright and brilliant to the minds of others so that they might be lifted up and become better than they were before. Speak words that make people's lives change. Speak words that bring courage so that the human soul can live, nations can be at peace with each other, and people can feel better about themselves. Speak life now and always in Jesus's mighty name.

Speak against negativity. Speak against murmuring and the negative things of this life by declaring the positive over the negative, the good over the evil, and the light over the darkness. Speak throne room prophetic words to this hopeless world, which is infected with violence, crime, racism, and injustice.

Speak God's divine, infallible words. Speak as His ambassador. Speak as His handiwork. Speak as His righteous masterpiece. Speak as His holy creation. Speak with your God-given ability to nations and give life to their once-dead dreams, visions, and revelations. Speak to the prime ministers, the presidents, and the dignitaries of this world and give them godly wisdom to live by and to rule their countries well.

Chapter 2

There Is No God Like You, Jehovah

God of the galaxy, I adore You in all ways possible. I bow to You, my Sovereign King of the universe. You are worthy of all my praise, worship, and adoration. I magnify You with all that is within me. There is no reservation in my praise, worship, and adoration to You Most High!

I call on You daily. My heart rejoices every minute of the day because of You. I stand in awe of Your untouchable name. I am awestruck by Your miraculous wonders. You change the galaxy like no other can. You are the creator of time, and You are in control of the heavens and the earth.

What a powerful God You are. Sometimes I am at a loss for words to describe who You really are. With my limited being, I try my best to utter with courage the name of the Trinity: God the Father, the Son, and the Holy Ghost. You are a wonder in the galaxy. You are marvelous. You are, in every sense of the word, awe-amazing. You cannot be overrun, overthrown, defeated, or duplicated.

You stand alone as God Almighty. You stand with your people as the difference maker. You stand with your chosen vessels of honor like a true heavenly Father. You give your remnants hope that will propel them to to higher dimensions. You are sought after by all the nations of this world.

Wow! Only you could be God. You have no end and no beginning. You are the master builder. You establish the foundation of the earth. You are the chief cornerstone. You step into every single situation and circumstance and leave Your footprint of hope in the hearts of Your people. You are the one true and living God. Make no mistake about this: You are my one true and only living God. You are God of the heavens and the earth.

God, I would be so lost without You in my life. You are the reason for my existence. You are the reason I am alive to write about Your goodness, greatness, love, compassion, and mercy toward an undeserving sinner who was saved by grace but is absolutely grateful for all that You have done in my life. Had it not been for You, the storms of life would have destroyed me. The waters that came to swallow me would have done just that. The failures of life would have caused me to crumble. My many disappointments would not have turned into divine appointments. My trials would not have turned into a gospel triumph. My hope would have become bleak.

But, God, You know when to step into my trials and tribulations. Thanks for being the center of my joy and life. Thanks for Your continual care, love, protection, and unfailing grace in my life. You are worth more to me than the entire galaxy, gold, silver, diamonds, and rubies. God, You are indescribable to me. Every day, I marvel, more and more, at Your everlasting goodness toward the children of men and me.

God, You are the glue that solidifies my life. You are the joy in my sorrow. You are the praise in my pain. You are my dance when I'm in mourning. You are the praise and deliverance weapons in my warfare. You are the roses that brighten all my days. You are the beautiful flowers that keep blooming daily in my heart. You are my peace in my sorrows. You are my goodness on my bad days. You are my gladness in my sadness. You are my anchor in my storm.

You catch me when I fall. You are my beautiful Rose of Sharon when I am fading. You are my steadfast, unshakable rock and firm foundation when mines crumble. You are my mountain mover when they stand tall before me. You are the defeater of all my giants. You are my fiery-furnace cooler when the heat is beyond bearable. You are my laughter when I cry. You are the bridge that helps me cross over my troubles with complete confidence.

I love You so much. I pour all my love out on You this day. I come to You today to give You praise. I come today to give You worship. I love You for who You are and not just for what I need. I want to express my sincere love for You, Jehovah. I rejoice in the God of my salvation. I rejoice because of Your holy name.

God, Your name is powerfully beautiful. Your name is sweetness in my mouth. Your name brings me so many blessings, joy, and laughter that

I have never had before. Your name brings such happiness in my spirit. God, Your name brings victory to every situation that is presented to you daily. Your name is a game and an atmosphere changer.

God, You have no rival, and that says it all. You stand through the ages as God and God alone!

Chapter 3

I Come to the High Courts of Heaven with My Petitions

In Jesus' mighty name, I come to the high courts of heaven with my petitions today. Father God, I lift up all my deepest concerns—the inner ones that I only share with You and that which touch the core of my heart. You know that the longing of my heart is to be one with You as You are one with your Father. I long to hold, taste, and see the countless promises fulfill in my life. I long to taste Your unending goodness, favor, and restoration. I long for Your persevering victory, breakthroughs, and deliverance. I long to run and not faint. I long to walk and not become weary.

I long to drink the living water, which will cause my heart to gloriously praise and worship You. I thirst for the living God, who owns the heavens and the earth. My soul pants for You, O Lord, as the deer pants for water. I have entered a stagnant zone, but on this day, I petition the high courts of heaven to move me to a place of relentless courage, boldness, and unstoppable anointing so that I can go to the third heaven. I come to the high courts of heaven so that I will storm the gates of hell and all that hell has against me. I come to the high courts of heaven to petition my case before God—whether it is known or unknown or revealed or concealed.

Jehovah God opens heaven's treasure rooms and pours out all of heaven's plans for my life and future. Yes, this journey is a battlefield, so I come to the highest court. This court's manifestations are beyond human's mere understanding and sight. Open my eye gate so that I can see all that heaven wants me to see. Open my ear gate and tell me heaven's profound, miraculous, transforming words. Open my mouth gate to speak as Your divine, created Oracle. Open the eyes of my understanding so that I am fully enlightened to the mandate of heaven; God's perfect will be done in my life, that others may see and know that Your light shines on me for good, always and forever.

High courts of heaven, all my hope is built on Your purposeful promises, which were spoken for my life before the earth even existed. My hope is wrapped up in Your potent, reliable Word. Your Word gives hope that I've never dreamed of. You created me so that I will be an anointed conduit on the earth. I will enjoy life and not simply endure it. Let me declare this once and forever: I am enjoying life and not merely enduring it. Cover me with the righteousness of Your right hand and clothed me with your righteousness and holiness.

In Jesus' mighty name, I come to the high courts of heaven so that I can deal with all the adversaries who are strong and lively. With the release of the Holy Ghost's power, I refuse to be defeated by my adversaries. Go ahead and release the heavenly anointing that will destroy all the yokes in my life. You are my all in all. You are the protective banner that covers me daily and forever on the earth.

In Jesus' powerful name, I come to the high courts of heaven with all my petitions so that I can move forward and never go backward. I want to move beyond my mere human understanding. Lord, I trust You wholeheartedly to lead the way. I will trust and obey. God, with my whole heart, I will follow hard after You. Lead me, Lord, and I will surely follow You. Lead me, Lord, for You will straighten the crooked paths before me. Lead me, Lord, by the hand and help me overcome all of life's obstacles that I face each new day. Lead me, Lord, and I will follow you into victory.

Father God, You never lose a fight. You have never lost a battle. You will always bring me out on the other side undefeated. God, You are my strong and mighty tower. You are my guiding light. For the rest of my life, lead me, Lord, and I will surely follow You. Don't ever leave my side. Don't ever let me go. God, without You, I will surely fail.

Be the light in my darkness. Be the moon in my midnight madness. Be my light when the storm clouds look dark. Shine through the clouds with your comfort. Shine through the clouds with Your unconditional love and unspeakable joy.

You are my champion of love. You are my judge in the courts of heaven. Therefore, humans' opinions of me don't shake my world. You are my balm in Gilead when I am sick. Yes, I declare and decree complete wholeness in my body, soul, mind, and spirit, right now in Jesus's mighty name. In Jesus's name, I declare right now that it is well with my soul. Yes, because Jesus's name carries weight. God has the final say in my life. God, You never fail and never end. You are never defeated but always reign. Yes, You are the reigning King of the universe. You are the great ambassador who will lead me through this world, guiding me gently to spread the gospel of Jesus Christ to all nations.

In Jesus' awesome name, I come to the high courts of heaven so that You will remove every spirit of limitation on my life. Now my territories and borders will be extended, giving me heaven's limitless authority, power, and dominion. In Jesus' righteous name, I come to the high courts of heaven so that You will remove every spirit of stagnation over my life, family, friends, and the ministry that you have called, anointed, appointed and chosen me to lead. In Jesus' holy name, I come to the highest courts in heaven for Your abundant life. It is not an empty life but a victorious one. My life will be an example to many who seek hope.

The thief cometh not, but for to steal, and to kill, and to destroy: I am come that they might have life, and that they might have it more abundantly. (John 10:10)

In Jesus' dynamic name, I come to the high courts of heaven to declare and decree this day and forever, that I shall not die but live to fulfill and inherit all the plans that God has for me.

> I shall not die, but live, and declare the works of the Lord. (Psalm 118:17)

> For I know the thoughts that I think toward you, saith the Lord, thoughts of peace, and not of evil, to give you an expected end. (Jeremiah 29:11)

God, in your bosom, I rest securely without worry and stress. In Jesus' glorious name, high courts of heaven, I come so that You will remove every negative word spoken over my life, family, friends, and ministry. I ask now, in Jesus's strong name, that You will release from heaven the spirit of positivity. God, send positive, strong, and courageous intercessors in my life, now and forever. God, send diligent, dedicated, and faithful workers into the vineyard. The harvest is now ripe and ready to be reaped, but the labourers are few. Lord, send labourers for the harvest.

In Jesus matchless name, I come to the high courts of heaven so that You will remove all the powers of darkness that come from Satan that fight against me daily. Release the Holy Ghost's power like never before in my life, Lord. Let it pour down harder and greater than the rain that falls from the heavens. Yes, God, let the Holy Ghost's power flow on me until I am absolutely soaked in You. I declare and decree that the spirit of limitations against me is now broken in Jesus strong name. I am moving forward with no limits, barriers, interferences, or interruptions.

In Jesus, healing name, I declare and decree that I am a wonder to many. I am a wonder to many that don't expect me to rise. I am a wonder to many that laugh at, mock and ridicule me. I am a wonder to those who said I wouldn't publish my books. I am a wonder to those who thought they would never see me rise above principalities, powers, and the rulers of darkness. Praise be to Almighty God that His promises for my life are yea and amen in Christ.

For all the promises of God in him are yea and in him Amen, unto the glory of God by us. (2 Corinthians 1:20)

What an awesome God You are. Your wonders amaze and dumbfounded me. You lift my head above the deep waters that Lucifer sends to drown me. You propel me with new life when Satan has his grave ready for me. You are my complete, deliverer, and restorer. I am eternally indebted to God for what He has done in my life. I commit my body, soul, mind, and spirit to God.

Jehovah God, I have placed my fruitful future and destiny in Your hands. At the cross of Jesus Christ, I now kneel. At the cross of Jesus Christ, I surrender my all to Jesus Christ. Jesus Christ shed His universal redemptive blood for all humanity. At the cross of Jesus Christ, I look and behold your power and glory. The cross of Jesus Christ upholds me and restores me daily. Indeed, my hallelujah belongs to Jesus. So I am giving all my hallelujah to You right now. I give my ultimate praise and worship right now to You in Jesus' awesome name.

Amazing God, You stand in front of me and take all of the Devil's blows that came from hell against me. To You, oh Lord, I am sincerely grateful. Jesus Christ blocks all of Satan's attacks. Lord Jesus, You jump over all my hurdles with me. God closed all the pits that await me. Lord, You quench all the fiery darts that the Devil meant for me. Lord, You heal all my sicknesses and diseases. You quenched my thirst and gave me Your living-healing water. Jesus Christ, You put barriers between my enemies and me so that they could not harm me. God, I am so thankful right now. I am so delighted. Truly, my soul magnifies You. My spirit exalts You, my God and my righteous King.

Jesus Christ, You straighten all my crooked paths. You gave me the light at the end of my darkest tunnel. You gave me beauty for useless ashes. Lord, You gave me a spirit of perseverance so that *quitting* will never be a word in my life's dictionary. Lord, You protected me from destruction, pestilence, and arrows that would have pierced me severely.

In Jesus' holy name, I declare and decree that Your blood is my perfect immunization against all contagious diseases in this world. I declare and decree that Your blood will save me from all airborne diseases and sicknesses in the mighty name of Jesus. I declare and decree that Jesus spotless blood is an amazing and transforming universal blood transfusion when needed in the most critical situation. The blood of Jesus Christ is not like other blood. It is uncontaminated, powerful, holy, pure, and rich. No human blood can be compared to the blood of Jesus. Jesus Christ blood is always fresh, reliable, and free for those who need deliverance and restoration from life's awful situations and circumstances.

All are welcome to receive Jesus Christ and obtain power from the blood of the spotless lamb. Come and receive it now. Freely the blood of Jesus Christ was shed for humanity's salvation. Freely, it is given to us when we ask for it. Confess and accept Jesus Christ as Lord and personal Saviour and receive Salvation. God will show up in your daily situations, just be still and know that He alone is Almighty God. He will hide you securely under His wings; so be still and know that He is God. Rest upon His breast and feel and enjoy deep comfort.

Heaven's high courts have all the answers to our life's problems. So we can come boldly and without hesitation and make our requests known unto God, our heavenly Father. The spirit of fear and doubt cannot enter into the high courts of heaven!

God, I now give You my unreserved praise, worship, and glory. I boldly declare and decree that I now move to the next dimension in You. I declare now that I will manifest the wonders of heaven in my life for Your glory. I rest in the hope of the second coming of Jesus Christ when there will be no more tears, sorrow, pain, death, stress, distress, suppression, oppression, or depression. I declare and decree that when you bring all your petitions to the high courts of heaven, believe that all the plans of God for your life will materialize. Our earthly courts have nothing on the highest courts of heaven, where God is seated as Ruler, King, and Priest above all else—to Jesus Christ, we will all bow to one day.

> That at the name of Jesus every knee should bow, of things in heaven, and things in earth, and things under the earth; (Philippians 2:10)

In the mighty name of Jesus, I come to the high courts of heaven requesting decisive victory, blessings, favor, healing, deliverance, signs, wonders, and miracles for my friends, family, and me.

Chapter 4

You Are Standing Upon the Rock, but Your Faith Is Still Wavering

I see that you are standing upon the Rock, but your faith is still wavering. You are standing physically, but your faith is in question. Yes, you are standing on the Rock of Ages. You cannot stand on the Rock of Ages without gaining a stronger faith in Christ Jesus. When you stand on the Rock of Ages, you must stand in confidence, authority, strength, stability, courage, boldness, and faith.

When you stand on the Rock of Ages, you will be able to withstand anything and be a winner. When you stand on the Rock of Ages, you are secure in Christ Jesus. When you stand on the Rock of Ages, all fears and doubts will flee, and your faith will rise to a higher dimension. You will soar higher than the eagles. Your eyes will see more clearly because the power of the Holy Ghost will remove the scales. You will be more rooted and grounded in the doctrine of Jesus Christ. You will have unshakeable faith. All strongholds around you will be broken because the Rock of Ages is our yoke breaker. When you are standing on the Rock of Ages, you are standing sure.

When you are standing on the Rock of Ages, you are steadfast and immovable; you are solid and strong, and you are firm. Have a solid grip and God's mercy, and goodness will hold you. God's awesome goodness and mercy will also follow you. Faith will guide you. Fellowship will embrace you. Comfort and loyalty will know you. Friendship will find you. Restoration will come to your address. Sweet songs of praise, worship, and deliverance will come forth. Victory is already yours by the power of the Rock of Ages. Your mountain will crumble and become as nothing before your eyes. Your dark days will end with the brightest light in the universe. Your sorrow will end, and the peace within you will be activated.

When you stand upon the Rock of Ages, you can do all anything in Jesus' mighty name. Your Jericho walls will come down, and you will embrace your moment of deliverance. When you stand on the Rock of Ages, your glory days are ahead of you. Your best life you will start to live now. Your gloomy days will end. You can taste victory and triumph in your mouth. You can see a brighter future ahead of you. You will gain a greater understanding of why some things that you prayed for didn't work out the way you thought they would because supernatural clarity is now given.

When you trust the Rock of Ages, He works things out better than you could have imagined. When you stand on the Rock of Ages, You automatically become a game changer in every situation and circumstance. Your negative perspective turns into positive. You are living without borders. You become a super blessing to many nations of this world. You are marked for success. You are a world changer with a paradigm-shifting mentality. You become a no-nonsense warrior, an unstoppable force to be reckoned with, a source of delight to many who walk on your path, and a source of encouragement to those who seek your advice. You are no longing living on the edge but supernaturally align. Your hope is ignited. You become a walking miracle that others look to for hope. Moments of despair no longer affect you. You have come out of your cocoon and are flying more beautifully than any butterfly.

When you trust the Rock of Ages laugher knows your name, victory enters all your platforms, and you are indeed an undefeated champion of hope in this world. There is no stopping you now. The Rock of Ages is on your side; therefore, you shall not die but live and declare the works of the Lord. You will live to fulfill the DNA promises that have been placed on your life before the foundation of the earth began. You are a unique gem. Your life will affect nations in positive ways. You are an influence that will speak to affluent people. You are a royal diadem.

When you declare God's potent word, it has life and power. Your word will help to shape the next generation. Your life is now enriched with love, peace, hope, joy, beauty, victory, comfort, healing, restoration, and deliverance.

God has given you the ability to overcome all of life's challenging obstacles. God has given you shining confidence. Your confidence is highly contagious. When you stand upon the Rock of Ages, the final say over your life comes from God Almighty!

Chapter 5

You Shall Leap over Walls and Run through the Enemy's Troops

What are you facing right now? Your present situations and circumstances will not be able to stop you from leaping over your walls and running through the enemy's troops. The power to do so is already inside you. You have the determination to fight like a courageous soldier. You can do all things through Christ that gives you the strength once you set your mind to do it. You will achieve greatness in this life, and you will not let anything or anyone stop you.

Go forth in Jesus mighty name, for you have already conquered the Jericho wall that stands before you. You have already run through the troops ahead of you. You are on the winning side. You are a bold, courageous, and mighty warrior for God.

You will not be stopped. You will not be hindered. You will not be interrupted. You will not be interfered with.

God is on your side, so you are definitely a winner. Stand on the winning side of life. There is no failure on the winning side. There is no such thing as *I can't* on the winning side. If you can believe it, you can surely achieve it.

You are on your mark, get set, and ready to trample your walls and run through the enemy's troops. There is no stopping you. Run on, victorious one. Your glory days will meet up with you. Don't look back and don't be distracted. Don't surrender. Don't give up. Don't give in. The path ahead of you is clear, with no obstacles in sight. Go forth in triumph, unstoppable gem.

Because of your fearlessness, you will see enemy troops as nothing more than stepping-stones. Because of your fierceness, you will see your walls simple to climb. Your tenacity will help you to be a true overcomer. Your power and will to live your best life is in view. The little bumps in the road of life are no match for the resilient person that you were created to be. You will withstand all the fiery darts that the enemy shoots at you.

The joy inside you will swell up and burst, releasing great hope and opportunities. Other people will be drawn to your great hope and will desire to know the secret of your unspeakable joy. I see that losing is not an option for you. So keep on going until you reach the finish line. You cannot go back now. You have come so far by faith and confidence. Now is not the time to look to the right or the left. Some people and situations come in our lives as real distractions but stay focused and you will win. Distractions come to sideswipe and derail your destiny!

Say goodbye to distractions once and for all. If you must, divorce distractions forever. Marry hope, confidence, victory, goodness, faithfulness, fidelity, loyalty, and commitment. While you are leaping over your walls and running through the enemy troops, avoid all detours. Detours are there to blindside you and often take you unaware and off course.

Stay in the race, be sober-minded as you run this race of life. Be alert.

Be wise and yet gentle. Don't pay attention to those who are running beside you. Stay in your lane. Try not to cross over to the other lanes. When you take your focus off your race and start watching the others that are running with you, this is a sure sign of competition, and it will take your focus off your race. Remember this: You are running to win. So don't focus on others. Each person will have to run his or her own life's race. Take your eyes off others. Keep your eyes on the prize that is ahead of you. If you fall, get right back up and keep on running. It's just a minor hurdle and will soon pass. You will still win in the end.

Whatever you do, keep hope alive and well inside your heart. Be determined to win this life's race. Go forth, move forward, advance, look up, and be positive. Stay in your lane. Keep in mind that you will not cross over onto someone else's lane. Crossing over someone else's lane will automatically disqualify you. You did not start this race or come this far to be disqualified. Take the word "disqualify" out of your life's dictionary.

You are a champion of hope who will give hope to this hopeless world. You are a champion of love who will give love to this loveless world. You are a champion of grace who will give grace to this graceless world. You are a champion of courage who will give courage to this frightening world. You are a champion of goodness who will give goodness to a world full of badness and sadness. You are a champion of encouragement to a world that desperately needs it.

You were born to give light, hope, and comfort. You were born to accomplish great things. You were born to stand out. You were born to be wiser than the wise, braver than the brave, and brighter than the bright.

Run on kingdom builders. Run on with God's force behind you. Run on with God's anointing, power, authority, and dominion, which has been invested within you. Run on kingdom soldiers, know that there are more for you than those who are fighting against you. Know this: In Jesus mighty name, the adversaries cannot win. The evil one stands no chance against you. The power of God within you is fierce, fiery, and firm. So stand fast in the liberty of Jesus Christ, our Lord.

> Finally, my brethren, be strong in the Lord, and in the power of his might. (Ephesians 6:10)

Wherefore seeing we also are compassed about with so great a cloud of witnesses, let us lay aside every weight and the sin which doth so easily beset us, and let us run with patience the race that is set before us, (Hebrews 12:1)

Chapter 6

Pressing through Frustration

Today, I come to encourage you to press through your frustration. Your situations and circumstances might seem to be insurmountable, but press on anyway. God is on your side. You will make it through. It may seem as if you are not making any progress in life, but press on anyway in Jesus' wonderful name.

Do what you were called to do. Do what you were created to do. Do what you do best, whether it is to sing, dance, preach, teach, paint, playing an instrument, or prophesy. Make a move to do it today. Yes, make a move, and fulfill your dreams. It won't just happen on its own. You have to tell yourself to run on with purpose and destiny. You will run with your dreams, visions, and revelations, which are deep inside of you and manifest them. You can do all things through Jesus Christ, our Lord. Lean on Him as your sure and blessed assurance. He will guide you all the way. God will not fail you. YOU CAN TRUST GOD!

> For this God is our God for ever and ever: he will be our guide even unto death. (Psalm 48:14)

God will be your GPS until the end of your life here on earth. God will not let you down, so run and be the best original you possible. Press on in spite of what comes your way. Some days will be harder than others. Some days you will feel like you can't go any further. You may feel overwhelmed to the point that hope is gone, and survival is nowhere in sight. You will get frustrated with your goals. Dig deep within you and pull out the strength that you need to push yourself again. You may slip and fall but remember that the righteous fall seven times and get right back up again. FEAR NOT-GOD IS THERE TO CATCH YOU WHEN YOU FALL!

> For a just man falleth seven times, and riseth up again: but the wicked shall fall into mischief. (Proverbs 24:16)

When you are going through life's greatest sadness, and despair, remember that you won't always have someone beside you to encourage you. At some point, you will have to believe in yourself and tell yourself that all things are possible if you only try. Never mind the many frustrations that come daily. They only come to distract you. Jump over your frustration with courage, confidence, and assurance. Learn to encourage yourself daily with the relevant word of God. Declare the holy word of God as your daily declarations over your life and believe them to be so. For example, say one of the following:

> I am a winner, and I must win.
>
> Almighty God fearfully and wonderfully made me.
>
> Failure is not an option, and I remove the word failure from my dictionary right now.
>
> I will not allow fear to hold me back. I will move forward into greatness.
>
> I will not allow frustration to hinder me from running my victorious race.
>
> I am a champion of hope.
>
> I will persevere, come what may.
>
> I will not look back or go back to the past, but I will move ahead to the glorious future that awaits me.

God is my refuge and strength. He will carry me all the way. He is my supernatural strength.

Where He leads me, I will follow Him because He will never lead me astray.

You can add to these list, or you can feel free to make your lists of declarations. Whatever you choose to do, declare, and believe that you are worthy of grace, greatness, goodness, love, restoration, deliverance, and peace.

You may have had a dream inside you since you were a child. Your heart may have desired this for a very long time, but every time you give it a try, you become frustrated and give up. I speak life to your mind, soul, body, and spirit. In Jesus mighty name, I renounce the spirit of setback and sabotage that rises against you. Arise in the mighty name of Jesus, and press on through your frustration. Great things and works have been produced and have been birthed by great people because they refuse to give up, but work through their frustrations.

So go forth in spite of what stands before you. Look at the long-term result and not the short-term. Look at the end and not the beginning. Look for the light at the end of the tunnel and not at the beginning. You can press on through frustration. You will make it. Life, itself, can get complicated and become frustrated but don't ever give up. Don't give in. Don't throw in the towel. Keep on trying. One day, you will win and see the great accomplishment that was made by you.

You might have been taking an exam and have failed it once or twice. That is no reason to quit. Tell yourself that quitting is not an option and that you are going to try again. You try again and pass. Hip, hip, hooray! All things are possible, even amid frustration.

Yes, I am aware that on some days, you might feel like it's your last day on earth because you are mentally, emotionally, physically, and spiritually drained, but stop and rest. Then start the next day again. Whatever you do, press on through the frustration, and you will come out as a winner. Keep a positive perspective, and you will see things on the brighter side. So when frustration comes to sideswipe you, this is another form of distraction that comes to derail your destiny. Don't let distractions conquer you, push ahead and be more than a conqueror. Tell yourself that fear is not a part of your destiny. GOD DID NOT CREATE YOU WITH THE SPIRIT OF FEAR!

For God hath not given us the spirit of fear; but of power, and of love, and of a sound mind. (2 Timothy 1:7)

I will not fear when frustration sets in. I will not fear even when everything around me is falling apart. I REFUSE TO WORRY AND BE AFRAID!

> The Lord is my light and my salvation; whom shall I fear? the Lord is the strength of my life; of whom shall I be afraid? When the wicked, even mine enemies and my foes, came upon me to eat up my flesh, they stumbled and fell. Though an host should encamp against me, my heart shall not fear: though war should rise against me, in this will I be confident. (Psalm 27:1–3)

Chapter 7

The "I Will" Promises of God in the Bible

The Bible is full of the "I will" promises of God, from Genesis to Revelation.

God's words are true. His promises in His Holy Bible are true. Read it to be enlightened. Read it to be wise and more powerful. Read it to gain greater insights each day. Read it to be empowered, mentally, physically, financially, emotionally, socially, psychologically, and spiritually. The Word of God is potent, relevant, reliable, trustworthy, active, sharp, quick, and incredible!

And I will establish my covenant between me and thee and thy seed after thee in their generations for an everlasting covenant, to be a God unto thee, and to thy seed after thee. (Genesis 17:7)

I will deliver him:

I will set him on high

I will answer him:

I will be with him in trouble;

I will deliver him, and honour him.

With long life will I satisfy him. (Psalm 91:14–16)

I will never leave thee, nor forsake thee. (Hebrews 13:5)

Fear thou not; for I am with thee: be not dismayed; for I am thy God: I will strengthen thee; yea,

I will help thee; yea, I will uphold thee with the right hand of my righteousness. For I the Lord thy God will hold thy right hand, saying unto thee, Fear not; I will help thee. Behold, I will make thee a new sharp threshing instrument having teeth: thou shalt thresh the mountains, and beat them small, and shalt make the hills as chaff. (Isaiah 41:10, 13, 15)

I will go before thee, and make the crooked places straight: I will break in pieces the gates of brass, and cut in sunder the bars of iron: And I will give thee the treasures of darkness, and hidden riches of secret places, that thou mayest know that I, the Lord, which call thee by thy name, am the God of Israel. (Isaiah 45:2–3)

Thou wilt keep him in perfect peace, whose mind is stayed on thee: because he trusteth in thee. (Isaiah 26:3)

Before I formed thee in the belly I knew thee; and before thou camest forth out of the womb I sanctified thee, and I ordained thee a prophet unto the nations. See, I have this day set thee over the nations and over the kingdoms, to root out, and to pull down, and to destroy, and to throw down, to build, and to plant. For, behold, I have made thee this day a defenced city, and an iron pillar, and brasen walls against the whole land, against the kings of Judah, against the princes thereof, against the priests thereof, and against the people of the land. And they shall fight against thee; but they shall not prevail against thee; for I am with thee, saith the Lord, to deliver thee. (Jeremiah 1:5, 10, 18–19)

And God said unto Moses, I Am That I Am: and he said, Thus shalt thou say unto the children of Israel, I Am hath sent me unto you. (Exodus 3:14)

And I will dwell among the children of Israel, and will be their God. (Exodus 29:45)

When thou passest through the waters, I will be with thee; and through the rivers, they shall not overflow thee: when thou walkest through the fire, thou shalt not be burned; neither shall the flame kindle upon thee. (Isaiah 43:2)

For I know the thoughts that I think toward you, saith the Lord, thoughts of peace, and not of evil, to give you an expected end. (Jeremiah 29:11)

And they shall be my people, and I will be their God: (Jeremiah 32:38)

But this thing commanded I them, saying, Obey my voice, and I will be your God, and ye shall be my people: and walk ye in all the ways that I have commanded you, that it may be well unto you. (Jeremiah 7:23)

At the same time, saith the Lord, will I be the God of all the families of Israel, and they shall be my people. (Jeremiah 31:1)

Hear, O my people, and I will speak; O Israel, and I will testify against thee: I am God, even thy God. (Psalm 50:7)

I am the Lord thy God, which brought thee out of the land of Egypt: open thy mouth wide, and I will fill it. (Psalm 81:10)

For this is the covenant that I will make with the house of Israel after those days, saith the Lord; I will put my laws into their mind, and write them in their hearts: and I will be to them a God, and they shall be to me a people: (Hebrews 8:10)

Therefore I say unto you, What things soever ye desire, when ye pray, believe that ye receive them, and ye shall have them. (Mark 11:24)

Be strong and of a good courage, fear not, nor be afraid of them: for the Lord thy God, he it is that doth go with thee; he will not fail thee, nor forsake thee. (Deuteronomy 31:6)

And I will bring them, and they shall dwell in the midst of Jerusalem: and they shall be my people, and I will be their God, in truth and in righteousness. (Zachariah 8:8)

Have not I commanded thee? Be strong and of a good courage; be not afraid, neither be thou dismayed: for the Lord thy God is with thee whithersoever thou goest. (Joshua 1:9)

And call upon me in the day of trouble: I will deliver thee, and thou shalt glorify me. (Psalm 50:15)

And what agreement hath the temple of God with idols? for ye are the temple of the living God; as God hath said, I will dwell in them, and walk in them; and I will be their God, and they shall be my people. (2 Corinthians 6:16)

He that overcometh, the same shall be clothed in white raiment; and I will not blot out his name out of the book of life, but I will confess his name before my Father, and before his angels. (Revelation 3:5)

And I will pray the Father, and he shall give you another Comforter, that he may abide with you for ever; (John 14:16)

But I will for their sakes remember the covenant of their ancestors, whom I brought forth out of the land of Egypt in the sight of the heathen, that I might be their God: I am the Lord. (Leviticus 26:45)

And I say unto you, Ask, and it shall be given you; seek, and ye shall find; knock, and it shall be opened unto you. (Luke 11:9)

I am Alpha and Omega, the beginning and the ending, saith the Lord, which is, and which was, and which is to come, the Almighty. (Revelation 1:8)

Chapter 8

Rise above Your Circumstances

It's a new day—a day filled with new hope, new peace, new joy, and new victory for you. Today is a gift from God. The fact that you are alive and reading this Devotional speaks for itself. Today, I write to encourage you to rise above your circumstances. Yes, you can rise above your circumstances, and you will. Tell yourself this is a new day to start over, to rebuild, to restore that which has been lost, and to start your new business ideas.

Right now, it may seem as if you are living your darkest day on earth. It might even feel like the darkest clouds are covering you. It might even feel like darkness surrounds you, and there isn't a way out.

Be encouraged. Rise up, dig deep within you, take courage, and find the spirit to fight. Dig deep within and take up perseverance, and you will be unstoppable. Dig deep within and take up the spirit of commitment, and you will not be stopped or hindered. You will never give up. Press on. Greatness is ahead of you, in spite of how dark it seems.

Right now, look at the horizon, and your perspective will change immediately. A new you will spring forth. Your best and brightest days are still ahead of you. You are strong. You are bold. You are brave. You are fierce and courageous!

Press on and push the darkness away from you. Press on and command the darkness to leave you. Press on and pray against the darkness. Fast and seek intervention against your darkness.

You have a winning spirit inside you. You have determination inside you. You are a determined eagle that will soar above your circumstances. You are a mighty giant who will not fall prey to your circumstances. No matter what life throws at you, you will rise above it and be the best you that you were originally created to be. You are uniquely you. You have what no one else on earth has. You can do what only you were created to do, and that is to impact the world and leave a lasting legacy for generations to come.

You may be facing a terminal disease, and all seems lost. I say to you this day that you can make it. Tell yourself, "I will get through this with the help of Almighty God, good friends, and family members." Claim restoration over your life right now in Jesus' mighty name. Don't give up because of what the doctor may have told you. Fight on, soldier of the cross of Jesus Christ. Tell yourself that you will beat this disease and live to write about it too. You will also give strength to those who are going through the same thing in their lives.

You might be trodden on but will come out victorious. Tell yourself that you are not a victim but God's victorious soldier. Whatever situations you are faced with right now, it will be over very soon, and you will see a brighter day. Don't focus on your circumstances but pray, seek support, and be positive about the outcome. Knowing that God is on your side is more than enough. Tell yourself that your darkest days are now behind you.

Today you might be facing marital issues. I say to you, don't give up. Life has its ups and its downs, but change is coming. The dawn is breaking in your life, and new beginnings are on the horizons. Work through your issues and cry if you must but don't give in to the pressure and quit. Seek counsel if you must, but don't ever give up on your marriage unless it becomes a toxic relationship. If you decide to move on, move forward as lessons learned and courage and confidence gained.

Let difficulties produce strong and true characteristics in you, such as patience, faithfulness, trustworthiness, perseverance, courage, faith, and so forth. Don't let difficulties derail your marriage. You will rise above it. Yes, you will soar above it. Yes, you will advance in it. You will overcome it and counsel others who are going through the same things you have been through. Rise above the conflicts in your marriage. Take effective communication classes that will catapult your marriage to new heights. Whatever you do, don't just give up or give in.

Whatever life throws at you today, you will rise above it by the power of His name. Jesus Christ's name is strong and mighty. He acts with might in all your circumstances. He is great, and He will triumph in all your battles. Stand strong. Hold fast. God is not through with you yet. You were born with greatness, and greatness and favor shall find you.

Rise above your circumstances because there is still much for you to accomplish in this life. The latter part of your life shall be greater. Don't let anyone or anything steal your desire to have the abundant life and pursue greatness in this life.

Be inspired. Be motivated. Be encouraged. Be empowered!

> Finally, my brethren, be strong in the Lord, and in the power of his might. Put on the whole armour of God, that ye may be able to stand against the wiles of the devil. For we wrestle not against flesh and blood, but against principalities, against powers, against the rulers of the darkness of this world, against spiritual wickedness in high places. (Ephesians 6:10–12)

> Knowing this, that the trying of your faith worketh patience. But let patience have her perfect work, that ye may be perfect and entire, wanting nothing. (James 1:3-4)

Chapter 9

When Feelings of Unworthiness Come to You, Tell Yourself that You Are Worthy

> But God commendeth his love toward us, in that, while we were yet sinners, Christ died for us. (Romans 5:8)
>
> But seek ye first the kingdom of God, and his righteousness; and all these things shall be added unto you. (Matthew 6:33)

When feelings of unworthiness come to you, tell yourself that you are worthy. There are times in our lives when feelings of unworthiness come into our minds. We then judge ourselves harshly. We feel a sense of failure. We also assess our lives, trying to see how much we have accomplished, and how far we have come. We beat ourselves up to the point of sorrow, which can sometimes lead to depression, oppression, and suppression.

This feeling of unworthiness will lead you to compare your life with others and to see if you can measure up. You are tempted to compete with the Joneses. Your thoughts run wild in negative ways, such as defeat, worthlessness, uselessness, downheartedness, insufficiency, incapability, not being able to measure up, hopelessness, and a deep desire to give up. The feelings of unworthiness can turn you into a competitive person—not in a good way!

Your mind, at this point, is no longer able to see things from a positive point of view. You look at other people's lives and wish you had what they had. A deep sense of jealousy and covetousness has entered your heart.

Feeling like you don't want to live can also come from a sense of unworthiness. A sense of unworthiness will leave you vulnerable to accept anything or anyone who comes into your life. The feelings that come with unworthiness can destroy your life. This sense of unworthiness can affect areas of your life, such as relational, social, physical, sexual, mental, psychological, and spiritual.

When you are feeling down, nothing looks positive. You cannot see the greatness that is waiting on the horizon for you. Your mind is temporarily cloudy. You are unfocused. Your attention span is very short. Your tolerance level is at a minimum. Your agenda has no future priorities. You are in deep despair as you wish and hope for a change.

There is a way to find hope in all of this. When feelings of unworthiness come to you, tell yourself that you are worthy. Yes, tell yourself that you are worthy. You deserve the best. Talk positively to yourself or give yourself daily declarations and affirmations that will help you combat this sense of unworthiness.

You are God's handiwork. You were created in His holy image. You were designed with greatness inside you. You will not be stopped. You will not be hindered. You will not accept the spirit of unworthiness but will accept worthiness. Yes, you are worthy of goodness, love, peace, joy, happiness, and excellence. You have what it takes to build your life positively.

Know this: You are not alone in your feeling of unworthiness. Many people experience this feeling. Even if they have made it big in society, they have encountered a sense of unworthiness at some point in their life's. However, they didn't let it stop them. They tell themselves they are worthy and move on.

I say to you right now; you are worthy. You are God's chosen, anointed, appointed, called, and selected saint. You are His end-time mouthpiece that will bring salvation and hope to a dying world. You are God's precious jewel that was made to fulfill a great destiny.

Your journey might be different from others whom you are comparing yourself to, but every person's journey is different. So embrace your own personal life's journey. Cherish who you are. Love yourself. Believe in yourself. Set goals for yourself and accomplish them step-by-step and one day at a time.

No matter what you are going through, tell yourself that you are worthy. When you declare worthiness over your life, it will give you the strength you never knew that you had. Tell yourself that life is worth living. Tell yourself that you are the righteousness of Almighty God. You are His royal diadem. You are destined to do great exploits in this life. Your final destination will be superb. You will leave a distinctive mark on society.

The worst thing you can ever do is compare your life's journey to someone else's. The competition will only lead you down the wrong destructive path. Be yourself. You are an original. You have gifts, talents, and creativity inside you that only you can manifest. Be the best you. You are rare. You are extraordinary. Dream big. Believe that all things are possible. Put away the spirit of pride. Seek help if you must. Seek support from family and friends.

God has big plans for you. Go after your dreams. Heaven is your limit. When you walk this life's journey with God, He will walk with you. He will carry you all the way and not just half of the way.

For I know the thoughts that I think toward you, saith the LORD, thoughts of peace, and not of evil, to give you an expected end. (Jeremiah 29:11)

You are courageous. You are a determined eagle. You will soar to unfathomable heights. You will discover new talents, gifts, and creativity that have always been inside of you. You will realize that you have more going for you than against you. You will rise up with an expectancy that good things will happen to you each day. You will not settle for second best, but the very best that life has to offer. You will see the glass as half full instead of half empty. You will see life from a positive standpoint.

You are worthy of any world stage. Don't look down on yourself. Let your self-esteem rise higher and higher each day. When feelings of unworthiness come, tell yourself that you are worthy!

Chapter 10

It's Extremely Important to Assess the People Who Come into Your Life

It's extremely important to assess the people who come into your life. Some relationships make or break your life. Assess people's characteristics and compatibility. It's vital to choose people who share the same or similar goals, dreams, visions, and passions that you have. Choose a compatible person that will help to catapult you into your destiny.

Assess people to see if they have negative or positive personality traits. A positive person can positively influence you, and a negative person can negatively affect you. Negative people will kill your dreams and destroy your destiny. So beware and look for early signs of it. If you see the spirit of negativity, don't ignore it and believe that it will go away on its own or that you can change people. Only God can transform the heart of people.

It's crucial that you make a list of the type of people that you will allow into your life. When you meet people, go to your checklist. Don't compromise what's on your list; otherwise, you will later regret that decision. When you compromise your checklist, you cause yourself undue stress, agonizing pain, hurt, and hardships. If you are not careful, you might also become bitter and resentful in the end.

Remember that we cannot change people. Some people are so set in their ways, and only God can transform them. You are not God. You are only human, and humans are fragile and finitely imperfect. Only God is infinitely perfect.

> There is a way which seemeth right unto a man, but the end thereof are the ways of death. (Proverbs 14:12)

> And Jesus said unto him, Why callest thou me good? there is none good but one, that is, God. (Mark 10:18)

Some people come into our lives as users, abusers, and deceivers. Be aware of the characteristics these three have. All three come with and have ulterior motives. It's all about what they can get from you and what they can gain from your life. They don't necessarily like you, but they will pretend that they are for you. They will stay with you for years until they have accomplished their hidden purposes.

We have many users in this world. They only call you when they have a need; otherwise, your phone will not ring. They know where and when to find you when they are in trouble. They are not sincere. Watch them carefully and be wise. Be careful how much you invest in their lives.

You need to know this about users: They honestly don't care about you. They don't have your best interests at heart. It's all about them. They are never happy about your accomplishments. They would rather that you listen to their accomplishments and celebrate them. As for you, they will never celebrate anything great or small in your life.

Be wise indeed about what dreams you share with them. They will even copy your dreams and try to fulfill them behind your back. They only give fake compliments. Don't be fooled by their charming ways. Their charming way is to trick you into believing that they are really in your corner, but deep down, they are not. Some users will say things like, "I am so happy for you or I truly love you," which is fake, or, "I am praying for you," which is a lie. Sometimes they say, "I wish you all the best," which is a deception, or, "I will do anything for you," when they are hypocrites.

Users come in different forms. They can even be your spouse, children, family members, or friends. Open your eyes and be careful of users. Users can sometimes damage your self-worth and your self-esteem. They can also damage you physically, emotionally, spiritually, mentally, socially, sexually, and financially. Don't become a victim to the users of this world. Walk away and never look back at them when you see red flags popping up.

Abusive people are deadly and have poison inside their hearts. They will do things to you that you can't imagine. This world has many abusers also. They will go to the extreme to hurt you physically, verbally, sexually, physiologically, financially, spiritually, mentally, and the list goes on.

You don't need to be around these kinds of people. You will not thrive or even survive around them. Being around abusive people can change who you are. Your nice personality can change into a nasty one. You can lose your self-worth. Once you lose your self-worth, you will start to feel unworthy. Abusive people are masters of pulling down others to make themselves look or feel good.

Run from them as fast as you can. Get help if needed. Speak to someone about your experiences. You might be surprised to learn that some of the people you share this with have gone through the same experiences and can be a great support to you.

Abusive people cannot see anything good in you. They won't encourage you to pursue the greatness that is within you. The impact of an abuser can leave you feeling that life is not worth living. However, I want to encourage you right now. You are worthy. You deserve good people in your life. You deserve people that will love, push, inspire, and motivate you to reach your destiny. Don't settle for less than the very best in this life. You only have one life to live, so live your best life now. Tomorrow might be too late. Draw strength from within yourself and walk away from abusive people.

Abusive people have many excuses for their disgusting behaviors. They will never take any responsibility for their actions. They always play the blame game. Abusive people are also great manipulators. They love to be in control of their environment and the people that are in their lives.

Don't feel guilty about their dreadful behaviors. When it comes to abusers, abusive people, don't ever try to justify their cruelty. Run for your life. You are worth more. You were born to win. You are a champion of hope, peace, joy, love, and goodness. You are destined for greatness. You were designed with talents, gifts, and creativity, which will help you pursue greatness in your life. So much more is ahead of you. You will no longer allow abusive people to put you down. You will rise above it. You will soar to unknown heights. You will make it. PRAY BIG. DREAM BIG. AIM BIG!

Deceivers are people that look handsome/beautiful, sometimes dress well, and have charming personalities. I call them devils in disguise. They come to steal, kill, and destroy your life. They are the greatest pretenders on this earth.

> Beware of false prophets, which come to you in sheep's clothing, but inwardly they are ravening wolves. (Matthew 7:15)
>
> The words of his mouth were smoother than butter, but war was in his heart: his words were softer than oil, yet were they drawn swords. (Psalm 55:21)
>
> The thief cometh not, but for to steal, and to kill, and to destroy: I am come that they might have life, and that they might have it more abundantly. (John 10:10)

They will pretend to be for you and to have your best interests at heart, but truly, this is not so. They enjoy saying things like, "I love you so much," and "I would never hurt you," but these words are lies from the pit of hell. These words best describe a deceiver: imitator, impersonator, fake, fraud, player, pretender, and shammer, to name just a few. These people are only out to do one thing—to destroy your life!

My advice is that you shouldn't be too desperate for people to come into your life. You have power over your life. Choose wisely who you let into your life. Use the gift of spiritual discernment to scope them out. Not everyone who appears friendly is really friendly. Check their actions and not their words. They are excellent at using words that you want to hear. Don't be too desperate for love because you might be taking on Mr. or Miss Wrong!

Be confident in yourself. Know what you want and don't want. Stand firm in your beliefs and don't compromise your goals. Learn how to achieve the spirit of contentment and use it well. Being content will help you to become wiser every day. I declare and decree right now in Jesus' mighty name that the Holy Spirit will release on you the Spirit of discernment and contentment!

Never give up on yourself. Never give up on your aspirations or goals in life. Never believe that good things will not happen to you. They will happen at the right time and season. Your patience will turn into delightful promotions!.

Refuse to accept people who are users, abusers, and deceivers. Don't second-guess yourself or veer off course to please other people. You already know, deep down, what to do. Let the Holy Spirit guide you. Trust and follow the path you are shown, one step at a time. Live your life one day at a time, YES you can do it and with confidence too.

FOLLOW YOUR GOD-GIVEN INTUITION!

Chapter 11

Guard-Your-Ears Gate

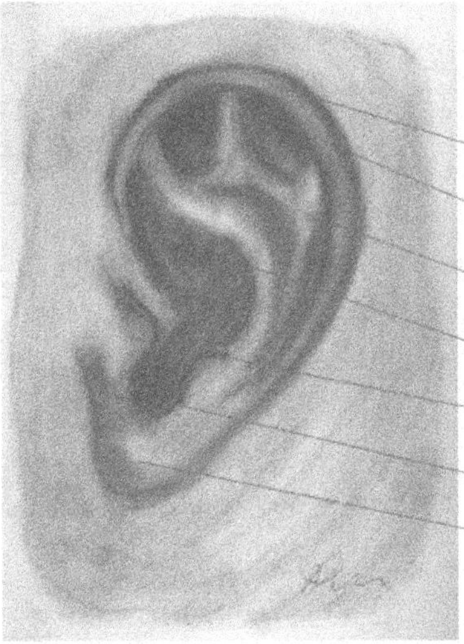

Incline your ear, and come unto me: hear, and your soul shall live; and I will make an everlasting covenant with you, even the sure mercies of David. (Isaiah 55:3)

But this thing commanded I them, saying, Obey my voice, and I will be your God, and ye shall be my people: and walk ye in all the ways that I have commanded you, that it may be well unto you. (Jeremiah 7:23)

I have heard of thee by the hearing of the ear: but now mine eye seeth thee. (Job 42:5)

We live in a world where profanity has become the norm. You can hear it on television, on social media, in music, at school, in homes, in marriages, in daycares, on the streets, in malls, in the workplaces, during your commute, in communities, and the world. People don't care where they say it. Profanity is spoken around babies, toddlers, children, youths, adults, and elderly. It is hard to go somewhere and not hear profanity. You can hear it when a boss speaks to his or her staff and vice versa. You can hear the vulgarity in the following interactions; with parents and children, in the schools between teachers and teachers, teachers and students, students and students, at home when husbands and wives speak, in the communities and all nations.

Profanity has become so normal in our present society that it's virtually hard to go anywhere and not hear it. I find this very disturbing. There needs to be a new level of self-respect and respect for each other in our society before the change can occur. Profanity is a form of disrespect, no matter how, why, when, or where it is spoken.

It's vital for you to guard your ears gate because when you hear profanity often, it can affect you. It can become part of you. Subconsciously, you continue to hear it in your head after you have been around someone who practices profanity religiously.

It is wise to daily detox your ears gate with the Word of God and the power of the Holy Spirit. Be conscious of what you allow to come into or pass through your ears gate. You are responsible for what you listen to and what you allow to pollute your spirit. Don't allow profanity to slowly eat away your inner joy, peace, happiness, goodness, laughter, and hope. Take control of your environment once you can do so. In other words, choose not to go to some places or around some people who practice profanity.

You can be the difference. You can make the difference. I am fully aware that we have to go to some places, such as work and school. In this case, try to filter out profanity when you hear it. What you hear through your ears gate can affect you mentally, sexually, emotionally, physically, socially, physiologically, spiritually, and so on.

Profanity can have a negative impact on your destiny. Be in control of your destiny. Tell yourself that you will not allow anyone to destroy your destiny. Others might think that you are strange or look like an oddball, but you have a choice about what comes through your ears gate.

Profanity has destroyed many homes, friendships, relationships, children, youths, families, and nations. It's important to educate our children and children's children about profanity because sadly, they are going to hear it one way or another. Teach your children what is normal and what is not. Teach your children to be careful about what they listen to. Daily, filter out the negative and embrace the positive. It's important that they know the difference.

What you hear doesn't stop at your ears. It seeps into your mind, soul, body, and spirit. If you are unaware of what you are listening to, after a while, you might find yourself partaking in profanity. Train your ears gate to allow positive messages in, whether it be by music, social media, sermons, inspirational and motivational messages, or other means.

You will become what you listen to. Your actions will reflect what you hear daily. Your attitude also reflects what you hear. So be careful what you listen to.

In your environment, you have more options as to what you and your family will listen to. Practice good mannerisms at home with your children so that when they go out into society, they will know how to adjust well and not be disturbed by profanity.

Today's children and youths are greatly influenced by many big-name celebrities that they see on television or social media. Many of them use profanity often, yet our children and youths still look up to them as great stars. As adults living in this world, we should be conscious of what we say in the hearing of children and youths because it has a great impact on their futures, in good or in bad ways. Be a positive role model that children and youths can admire. You don't need to utter profanity to be cool. Be wise, intelligent, and be you!

Not that which goeth into the mouth defileth a man; but that which cometh out of the mouth, this defileth a man. (Matthew 15:11)

> Death and life are in the power of the tongue: and they that love it shall eat the fruit thereof. (Proverbs 18:21)

As adults living in this world, we should all want to protect our children and youths. Why? They are the future generation. They are the next prime ministers, presidents, mayors, premiers, doctors, lawyers, nurses, priests, police officers, judges, and the list goes on. They need to have sober minds, bodies, souls, and spirits to master their callings, gifts, and talents.

Profanity can make or break you. It can shake or mold you. It can cause you to leap forward or to become stagnant in life.

Being able to hear is a beautiful gift. Having the ability to hear with compassion is a superb blessing, which some people in this world don't have. We should be so grateful for the gift of hearing.

Most people with hearing loss wish that they could hear, so be thankful that you can. Don't take your ability to hear for granted. You will never know how it affects you until it is gone. So each day, get out of bed and say, "Thank You, Lord. I can hear today, and today will be a great day, and I am blessed divinely with the ability to hear." Be thankful that you are not deaf. Appreciate the ability to hear more and more each day.

Think about this for a moment: If you have sudden hearing loss, how would you feel? Would you regret that you hadn't cherished the ability to hear? Would you have more compassion for deaf people in our society? How would you react if you learned that you could no longer hear? Take five minutes to answer these questions. After you have answered these question; I believe you will develop an attitude of gratitude. You will be more compassionate to those who are deaf.

Those that can hear should guard their ears gates. Be selective of what you allow to come into your ears. Choose what to reject and what to accept.

The ears not only provide the ability to ear but also make it possible for us to maintain our balance. We also need to be careful about who we listen to.

Be sober, be vigilant; because your adversary the devil, as a roaring lion, walketh about, seeking whom he may devour: (1 Peter 5:8)

> Submit yourselves therefore to God. Resist the devil, and he will flee from you. (James 4:7)

Also, be careful about how you listen because good listeners make good company. Good listeners make good friends. Good listeners make good teachers. Good listeners make good counselors. Those who don't listen do most of the talking. They usually have the final say. So learning how to be an excellent listener is very important.

> Out of heaven he made thee to hear his voice, that he might instruct thee: and upon earth he shewed thee his great fire; and thou heardest his words out of the midst of the fire. (Deuteronomy 4:36)

The way you listen is vital. Be careful not to listen superficially or emotionally. Be wise and don't listen with self-centeredness.

Listening is an art. Seek wise people to demonstrate it for you. As Christians, we live in this world but are not to be like this world. Don't listen, worldly. Listen to the things of God, to things that will advance your life, to things that will edify you, and to things that will cause tremendous growth in your life.

What you hear can deeply affect your heart negatively or positively. So be careful what you allow to come through your ears gate.

> He that hath ears to hear, let him hear. (Matthew 11:15)

As Christians, how we listen to the Word of God matters. How we listen to and receive the unadulterated Word of God as it is preached to us will greatly impact our Christian maturity and fruitfulness. Jesus Christ commanded that we, as Christians, be active listeners and not passive ones. So activate your listening skills right now in Jesus' mighty name. The way unbelievers listen is also very important because it can bring about salvation, transformation, conversion, deliverance, breakthroughs, and so much more.

Believers and nonbelievers need to be aware of the many distractions in their daily lives, which hinder them from receiving the Word of God. Daily, fight the spirit of distraction for yourself and others. Distractions can hinder your walk with the Lord. It can stunt your growth process. Before we listen, we should prepare our minds, souls, bodies, and spirits to receive messages that will be conveyed to us.

> But the tongue can no man tame; it is an unruly evil, full of deadly poison. (James 3:8)

Profanity has greatly impacted our society in unbelievable ways. It is a normal way of life for some people. It is how they live. Social media sites seem to draw a great deal of profanity out of people. On Social media, quite often people don't see each other face-to-face, so it's easier to hide behind their screens to express themselves to the world by using profanity.

It's important for believers to guard their speech throughout the day. Swearing and cursing can also be seen on many television shows and in movies. You can choose what you and your children watch and don't watch. Be sensible and sensitive about your choices when it comes to what goes through your ears gate.

Swearing is as old as the human race. The Bible gives us examples of people who swore. In today's society, cursing and swearing fill the air all around us.

> Then said I, Woe is me! for I am undone; because I am a man of unclean lips, and I dwell in the midst of a people of unclean lips: for mine eyes have seen the King, the Lord of hosts. (Isaiah 6:5)

> But I say unto you, swear not at all; neither by heaven; for it is God's throne: (Matthew 5:34)

> But I say unto you which hear, Love your enemies, do good to them which hate you, Bless them that curse you, and pray for them which despitefully use you. (Luke 6:27–28)

> Thou shalt not take the name of the Lord thy God in vain; for the Lord will not hold him guiltless that taketh his name in vain. (Exodus 20:7)

Please read the Ten Commandments. The Ten Commandments are codified in Exodus 20 and Deuteronomy 5. Jesus, in His potent and holy words, reminds us not to use swearing or cursing words to demean another person (see Matthew 5:21–22). Let's take our example from Philippians.

> Finally, brethren, whatsoever things are true, whatsoever things are honest, whatsoever things are just, whatsoever things are pure, whatsoever things are lovely, whatsoever

things are of good report; if there be any virtue, and if there be any praise, think on these things. Those things, which ye have both learned, and received, and heard, and seen in me, do: and the God of peace shall be with you. (Philippians 4:8–9)

Chapter 12

Heaven Holds the Secret for Your Life: Pain, Heartbreak, Hurt, and Disappointments

Heaven holds the secret for your life: Pain, heartbreak, hurt, and disappointments. Life may have knocked you down many times. Life may seem dull and as if nothing is going to happen for you. You may feel like giving up. You may feel like throw in the towel. Everything around you seems to be defeated. You may feel like a victim and not a victor. People may not be a source of encouragement when you need it most. All hell is breaking loose, and you are standing on the brink of hopelessness, ready to end the fight of life.

I am here to speak to you right where you are. Yes, your life may not look good, and things may not seem attainable right now in the natural world. But if you can switch your focus and begin to believe what I am going to tell you, it will change the course of your destiny. Heaven holds the secret for your life. Heaven wants you to know that what God has in store for your future far supersedes all that you see with your natural eyes. Your latter years will be greater than your former ones. Heaven is not counting your mistakes and failures. God has your back, your best interests at heart, and is waiting and ready to share them with you. Victory is ahead of you. Hold fast. Press hard on life's accelerator and keep moving forward to a brighter future.

Heaven wants you to know that yes, your life will turn out beautiful. Your life will be a force to be reckoned with. Your life will be unstoppable. Your life is marked for success and greatness. Your name will be a household name. Many memorials will be established in your name.

Your heartbreak will mend. Your heartbreak was only a process that God was taking you through. Endure the process because it will soon be over, and you will see why you had to go through it. It will make a better you—a you that will stand strong, bold, wise, and courageous than you can ever imagine. Your heartbreak will become a great lesson you have learned.

Right now, you might be hurting so bad that you feel like end it all. Don't end your life because new beginnings await you on the horizon. New hope is bursting out of heaven for you. New love is shining from heaven to you. New relationships are coming your way. New friendships are your portion. Laughter will be your daily meal. Brightness will be your apparel. Heaven is smiling down on you with excellent ideas, inventions, and innovations. You cannot give up now because too much is at stake. You haven't lived your best life yet. Don't ever, ever, ever give up. Don't ever give up!

The devil is a liar. Your feelings of hurt will soon pass away and be remembered no more. Joy is coming to you in abundance. Your blessings are coming to you from heaven like the abundance of rain. You will see the goodness of the Lord in the land of the living. You will see that all you have been through was worth it. You will become so empowered that you will empower others who are going through what you have been through.

Heaven has your back. Heaven will download your future successes.

Heaven has all you need to thrive and survive. Be of good courage. You are not alone. Your darkest moments may seem to be the longest, but the divine purpose is being birthed out of them. Whatever you do, don't ever, ever, ever give up. It will be worth your wait. Take courage. Have faith!

Dig deep inside you, and you will find the strength that you need to carry on. You will find a source of hope that will brighten your day. You will find peace amid hurt, heartbreak, and disappointments. You will find that the healer and miracle worker is at work on your behalf. His name is Jesus Christ of Nazareth. Don't be ashamed to call on Jesus Christ for help at any given time. He is available 24-7. He knows your beginning and your end. He gives life and takes it. He alone is the author and finisher of our faith.

> Looking unto Jesus the author and finisher of our faith; who for the joy that was set before him endured the cross, despising the shame, and is set down at the right hand of the throne of God. (Hebrews 12:2)

Right now, you may be feeling disappointed in people, your job, your marriage, your children, and so forth, but if you start to believe again, God can and will turn your disappointments into blessed appointments. Sometimes it's hard to make sense of your disappointments. Sometimes it's hard to fathom what is really going on. Every time you hope for an outcome, the opposite happens to you. You cannot comprehend this. You sometimes have to give a big sigh and release your heart!

I speak to you as a person who has been where you are now. I had to turn all my focus on God, who controls the heavens and the earth before I could receive the answer to my disappointments. I discovered that heaven truly held all the secrets for all my disappointments. Heaven consoled me in ways no one else could. Heaven told me that all things that seemed like disappointments in my eyes were not disappointments in God's eyes. God reminded me not to see things in the natural but in the supernatural. TEARS DO SPEAK!

When we walk in the spirit and not in our flesh, our flesh becomes weaker, and our spirit within us grow stronger. Galatians 5:16–18 declares,

"This I say then, Walk in the Spirit, and ye shall not fulfill the lust of the flesh. For the flesh lusteth against the Spirit, and the Spirit against the flesh: and these are contrary the one to the other: so that ye cannot do the things that ye would. But if ye be led of the Spirit, ye are not under the law."

I use to see all my disappointments through the eyes of the flesh and not through the eyes of the spirit. When this reality awakened me, and what heaven had revealed to me, I cried and asked for forgiveness. I was faced with a specific situation. I prayed and asked God to work it out in my favor, but the opposite thing happened. At first, I started to cry and feel despondent. I even became discouraged for a short while. The answer I was looking for was YES because that was what my heart, soul, mind, body, and spirit wanted to hear, but God had a different answer. God's answer was NO. Stay strong and keep the faith even when the answer from God is NO. Heaven spoke back to me with the following message:

> "My daughter, if I really gave you what you thought you wanted, I would not be giving you My best. Your best is not My best. This situation is no match for what I have in store for you. This situation turned out the way it did so that I can better align you to your greater destiny in Me. If I had given you what you thought was the best for you, your destiny would have ruined. Your desire to carry the unadulterated gospel of Jesus Christ would be null and void. Your inspiration in Me would come to nought. You would have zero joy right now. You would not have such triumphant victory that you are having now. You would have seen many dark days of great sorrow and ashes. I, God, saved you from this by allowing you to be disappointed, even though it has hurt you a bit. But if I had not done this for you, you would be living in total misery. I, God, know the future, and know what is best for your future. I promised only good and perfect gifts and nothing less. Read Jeremiah 29:11; James 1:17; and Proverbs 19:21."

I began to thank God more and more for blocking what I thought was good for me. I praised Him that He intervene on my behalf. In those moments, I realized how much my heavenly Father loves me and sincerely cares about every detail of my life—enough to not let me have my own way, which would have destroyed my destiny in Him!

> For my thoughts are not your thoughts, neither are your ways my ways, saith the LORD. For as the heavens are higher than the earth, so are my ways higher than your ways, and my thoughts than your thoughts. (Isaiah 55:8–9)

God also comforted me throughout my disappointments by drawing me to Romans 8:28, which declares, "And we know that all things work together for good to them that love God, to them who are the called according to his purpose." At first, I could not see the fullness of this scripture until I pulled it apart, word by word. Suddenly, the Holy Ghost revelatory light shined volumes on it. Instantly, I gained knowledge, wisdom, and understanding!

Praise be to God for His infinite wisdom in my life today. I now give thanks to Him for all of life's heartbreaks, hurts, setbacks, and disappointments. My hope is steadfast in Him. He knows what is best for me. I am trusting my Savior more than ever to lead, guide, and protect my every step in this life. I ask Him daily to go before me and straighten all the crooked paths. I say, "Yes, Lord, lead me on the path that You have destined for me." God surely does all things best, even when my finite mind doesn't always comprehend it. I now trust His process for my life. I encourage you to do the same thing for your life!

> Declaring the end from the beginning, and from ancient times the things that are not yet done, saying, My counsel shall stand, and I will do all my pleasure: (Isaiah 46:10)

Chapter 13

When You Stay in the Secret Place, Visions Are Made Clear

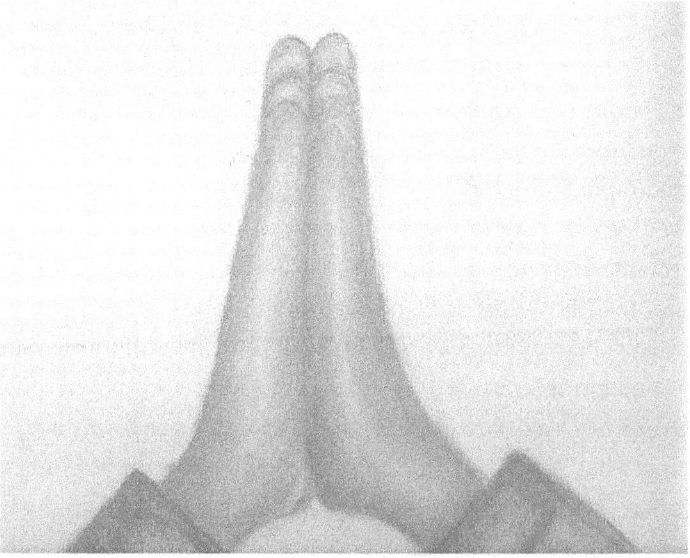

He that dwelleth in the secret place of the most High shall abide under the shadow of the Almighty. I will say of the LORD, He is my refuge and my fortress: my God; in him will I trust. Surely he shall deliver thee from the snare of the fowler, and from the noisome pestilence. He shall cover thee with his feathers, and under his wings shalt thou trust: his truth shall be thy shield and buckler.

> Thou shalt not be afraid for the terror by night; nor for the arrow that flieth by day; (Psalm 91:1–5)

The term "secret place" appears in the Old and New Testaments and often refers to the way our soul is in a relationship with the Sovereign God. We can get to the secret place by first having a spiritual relationship with God. First, by reading and believe Romans 10:9 which declares; "That if thou shalt confess with thy mouth the Lord Jesus, and shalt believe in thine heart that God hath raised him from the dead, thou shalt be saved." Once you accept Jesus Christ as Lord, you are now in a relationship with God. You then have access to His secret place. When you stay in the secret place of God, your dreams and visions are made clear. God has great and beautiful plans for your life. He is working out all of the details. He is actively doing all that is within His power on your behalf. He knows the process that He must allow you to go through. He knows the beginning from the end. He is fighting all your battles. He creates beautiful things out of your messy clay. He is more than able to mold, fashion, reshape, align, and reposition you!

Dwelling in the secret place of Almighty God brings such contentment. It brings healing, peace, joy, deliverance, hope, victory, laughter, breakthroughs, and so much more. God's secret place will help you discover the real purpose of your life. Your life will immediately take on a new meaning. Your will to live will become so much stronger than before. Your heart's desire is to do God's will and not your own.

Things that appeared dim now shine with the light of God on them. Things that were once hopeless become hopeful. Things that were dead now come alive again. You will experience His resurrection power in your life and new desires to pursue, overtake, and recover. You will experience new beginnings that will manifest daily in your life. You will experience the birthing of your dreams, visions, and revelations. You will be at a place where it is easier to accept first the love of God and then accept love from the people who are around you.

The secret place gives new confidence and strength to move forward and to fulfill your lifelong dreams and visions. God Almighty can more easily order your steps when you dwell in the secret place. Your failures are forgotten, and forgiveness is birthed anew within you. You can freely forgive others for the wrongs they have done to you and vice versa because forgiveness flows out of love, and love flows out of knowing you have been set free. Complete forgiveness is called complete freedom. You will love your neighbor as yourself. You will love the unlovable, the unreachable, the downcast, and outcasts of society.

In the secret place of Almighty God, your visions are made clear because God reveals His perfect will and plans for your life in ways that are easy to follow. Your imperfect thoughts become His thoughts, and your imperfect ways line up with His perfect ways. You will, at this point, become pliable in His hands. He is then able to do what no other power can do. In the secret place of Almighty God, He will tell you things that you never knew. Hearing God speaks to you is like experiencing a new birth in Christ.

The original mandate that God has upon your life before the foundation of the earth will make more sense. You are God's original masterpiece. The enemy can not duplicate your DNA. Satan can no longer speak lies to you and have you believe them, once you are in the secret place. Why? In the secret place of Almighty God, you gain supernatural, overcoming power to destroy all powers of evil and darkness. You are unstoppable in your pursuit of greatness in your life. You are who God created you to be and will become all that God said that you would be. You will recognize that you are worth far more than what you have settled for. Your worth is far above gold, silver, bronze, rubies, or diamond. You have God's power to control the good or bad things that will come into your life. You will have an urgency to make contact with people who have the same mindset. People who dwell in the secret place can relate to you much better. Deep calleth unto deep. Psalm 42:7: "Deep calleth unto deep at the noise of thy waterspouts: all thy waves and thy billows are gone over me."

In the secret place, God is your partner in prayers. More power is in your prayer. Your gifts are more effective, and powerful demonstrations of your gifts become evident. Your ability to preach and teach the unadulterated Word of God becomes stronger, and signs, wonders, and miracles accompany it. The Holy Ghost will unction you to function!

1 John 2:20: "But ye have an unction from the Holy One, and ye know all things."

Dwelling in the secret place of Almighty-God brings comfort to any wounded soul. He is a heart mender and a comforter when all hell is breaking loose in your life. He is an activator of the gifts, callings, and ministries that are within you. You are more anointed because you now have a heavenly, divine connection to the throne room of grace. No demon can stop you. God is always for you. He is always on your side, looking out for your better good. The Lord is your greatest weapon that fights on your behalf while you fast, and pray in His dwelling place. You will truly learn how to be still and know that He is God. You will have more testimonies of praise to share with the nations. You will have a spirit of gratitude to God for the goodness and mercy He has shown to you. The spirit of complaint will be no more within you. You will testify surely and gladly of God's great wonders toward you daily.

Dwelling in the secret place of Almighty God helps you discover your heavenly heritage, which was allotted to you before the foundation of the earth began. Heaven is your rightful inheritance. Cherish it, live it, and hope for the day of Jesus Christ's return. You will get rest from the wicked. Your soul will have complete peace and everlasting joy. No one can trouble you anymore. You can look forward to freedom from the cares of this life, which so daily perplex us. No sorrow, sickness, death, or tears will be there. There will be no more nights because God Himself is Light of all lights. He is the Bright Morning Star. He is and will remain the reigning champion of all time.

Specific guidance is given in the secret place of Almighty God—guidance about marriage, relationships, business, children, your next goal, school, your job, and so much more. You don't need to fret anymore about your next move. He will let you know what His next move is for your life. He will grant you success. Your plans will never fail because they are His perfect plans for your life. Your joy will not be withered because it is His perfect, unspeakable joy.

In the secret place, God's love for you will become undeniable and unconditionally real. He will create impossible ways for you and open extraordinary doors that no one else can open for you. He will reign as God Immortal, Invisible, and the Only Wise, True, and Living God. He is the rock who anchors your soul. He is the bishop of your soul. He becomes the love that you never experienced before. He is unchangeable. Praise be unto the Most High God. Lord, Your name is worthy to be praised. Lord,

I praise you from the bottom of my heart. My praise is bubbling up from deep inside me because I am dwelling daily in your secret place.

When you dwell in the secret place, you gain a new love for God. You have a deeper desire to praise and worship Him often. The relationship between you and God grows stronger and sweeter every day. Your praise for God exalts Him higher. Your worship of Him is greater. You depend on God for all your needs. Your acts of obedience are so easy. You will never be ashamed to share with the world the hope you have in Christ Jesus.

> Delight thyself also in the Lord: and he shall give thee the desires of thine heart. (Psalm 37:4)

In the secret place, new songs are birthed within your spirit, which allows you to sing unto Him a new song every day. Glory to the Most-High King. Jesus Christ is King of the ages. He is King of all kings and Lord of all lords. He is indeed called Abba Father. He loves, comforts, blesses, heals, forgives, restores, and soothes like no other. He alone is God!

> For thou art great, and doest wondrous things: thou art God alone. (Psalm 86:10)

No matter what evil things have happened in your life, know that once you enter into God's secret place, your past is forgotten, and your future has begun. A new page of hope and hopeful events becomes your story of hope. It will also encourage others. All things are possible in God's secret place. What might seem impossible for you to achieve has now become possible because God's secret place is a place of grace. God's secret place is where you can start over again and fulfill all your dreams, visions, and revelations.

By dwelling in the secret place of God almighty, you no longer live in Lodebar—a place of not having. You will no longer lack anything because you will understand Psalm 23:1 and Philippians 4:19 better. God can provide all your daily needs.

> The Lord is my shepherd; I shall not want. (Psalm 23:1)

> But my God shall supply all your need according to his riches in glory by Christ Jesus. (Philippians 4:19)

Your household will rise and call you blessed when you are dwelling in the secret place. You will become a lender to many nations and will not borrow from any. Your storage basket will always overflow. Favor will follow you. Success shall know your name. Blessings will become your portion. Prosperity is your new norm!

Psalm 91 encourages us to dwell sweetly in His secret place, for all we need in our lives is provided there. God's deliverance will show up on your behalf in His secret place. What He did for King David, he can do for you. Our strength, restoration, and deliverance are birthed out of God's secret place. We automatically become stronger and mature as we dwell in the secret place. We grow stronger in faith. Great protection is found in God's secret place. In the secret place, you can be assured that Isaiah 54:17 is real, and you are covered by it.

> Isaiah 54: 17: "No weapon that is formed against thee shall prosper; and every tongue that shall rise against thee in judgment thou shalt condemn. This is the heritage of the servants of the Lord, and their righteousness is of me, saith the Lord."

Chapter 14

When the Creator Made You, He Put No Limits on You

It is as high as heaven; what canst thou do? deeper than hell; what canst thou know? (Job 11:8)

In the same day the Lord made a covenant with Abram, saying, Unto thy seed have I given this land, from the river of Egypt unto the great river, the river Euphrates: (Genesis 15:18)

> Every place that the sole of your foot shall tread upon, that have I given unto you, as I said unto Moses. (Joshua 1:3)

> So God created man in his own image, in the image of God created he him; male and female created he them. (Genesis 1:27)

When the Creator made you, He put no limits on you. No matter what life dictates to you that doesn't line up with the promises of God, this will come to an end once the Holy Spirit has enlightened you. Right now, hell is causing havoc in the lives of your children, your spouse, your coworkers, and you. Know this today: When God created you, he didn't put any limits on you.

What does this mean? It means you can do all things, including impossible things. Only heaven is the limit to what you can and will achieve in your life. Because your Creator didn't put any limits on you, let no one stop you. Let no one interfere with your destiny. Don't allow the naysayers of this world to put limitations on your life. Don't let a negative mindset hold you back from achieving all that the Creator has in store for you before the foundation of the earth. When the Creator made you, He built you with everything you would need so that you could fight and win. Nothing was or is short in your life. Just move forward, believe in yourself, and fulfill your God-given destiny.

The sky is not your limit. Heaven is your limit. Because God places no limits on you, this means your destiny is limitless. You will achieve all that your Creator has destined for your life. Don't allow society or your environment to dictate what you can and cannot do. I say to you once more that you can and will achieve all things. Did you know that your Creator made you with characteristics such as strength, courage, boldness, confidence, bravery, victory, power, prosperity, and success? Let me reassure you: YES, HE DID!

You have the strength needed to stand up and fight the giants that are in front of you today. Yes, as you fight your giants, know that they will fall in front of you. God will give you His courage. You will have strength like Samson had. You have the courage you need to overcome all obstacles, to leap over walls, and to run through the enemy's troops without fear. Yes, you do have the Holy Spirit power inside you. Activate it, move forward, and fulfill your destiny. Your courage will become like that of Joshua, who was a great commander, and of Abraham, who did what God told him to do without wavering.

You have the needed boldness to face your adversaries and to win because you are on the winning side. Having boldness gives you the upper hand all the time. God didn't give you the spirit of fear.

> For God hath not given us the spirit of fear; but of power, and of love, and of a sound mind. (2 Timothy 1:7)

You will possess boldness like the prophet Elijah. Like King David, you too have the needed confidence and courage to go into the enemy's camp and take back what rightly belongs to you. You will go in, recover, restore, and gain blessings, that has already been assigned to you. You will follow the instructions of your Creator and win by a landslide. You will become God's warrior and champion as King David.

You have the bravery needed to fight all of your spiritual battles. You will come out on the winning side. You will be like Queen Esther. The bravery of God in your life will help you to defend God's people, hands down strategically.

> Blessed be the LORD my strength which teacheth my hands to war, and my fingers to fight: (Psalm 144:1)

You have the victory inside you that will cause you to wave your banner high in all of life's situations and circumstances. The battles you now fight will become easier because you left them in the hands of your Creator. He is the undefeated champion of all time.

You have the power you need to be an ambassador to nations. Like Moses, who delivered the children of Israel, you will be used to deliver many nations. Your Creator gave you His Dunamis power. This power has come out of Jesus Christ's resurrection. All your Red Seas will part by the power of the Holy Ghost. Your creator has no rival.

> And Israel saw that great work which the LORD did upon the Egyptians: and the people feared the LORD, and believed the LORD, and his servant Moses. (Exodus 14:31)

You have great power like Moses, who was the greatest leader of Israel. He was unstoppable. He was fierce. He was hopeful for his people. Moses had no limits on his life, and neither are you.

You have the anointing and prosperity of the Holy Ghost needed to perform signs, wonders, and miracles by the hand of your Creator. He has already given you the needed victory to bring forth His matchless glory in the earth. You have wisdom and riches like King Solomon. King Solomon built the most beautiful temple for his Creator, and your Creator will give you the knowledge to gain wealth, and divine instructions to build His kingdom and also to catapult your life. You are more than capable of building it too. You are equipped by God to achieve all things.

> So king Solomon exceeded all the kings of the earth for riches and for wisdom. (1 Kings 10:23)

You have the needed success to carry out God's promises. His many promises for your life start in the book of Genesis and goes all the way to Revelation. Even when the enemy is fighting hard against you, defeat is not an option. The defeat was never in your DNA, to start with. Push ahead right now. Start working on your dreams. Start working on the countless visions and revelations that are dormant inside you. You will be like Joseph. Your delays will be gracious comebacks!

> But as for you, ye thought evil against me; but God meant it unto good, to bring to pass, as it is this day, to save much people alive. (Genesis 50:20)

When the Creator made you, He didn't put any limits on you. I say to you this day, take the limits that you have placed on your life and throw them in the bottomless pit of hell. Don't allow this world to influence what God has put inside you. Don't shy away from being all that you were created to be.

You were born to win. You were born with enormous blessings and favors on your life. Tap into the reservoir of God's goodness. Step into the reservoir of God's undeniable greatness for your life. Step into the deep by activating your God-given faith. Come out of your comfort zone and replace it with advancements. It's time for you to move deeper into the spirit of God. It's time to see from your Creator's perspective what He has in store for those who love Him.

Get out of your mediocrity and move into God's democracy. It's time to take a giant leap of faith and manifest your gifts, talents, and calling in God. You are limitless. You have the freedom to achieve all things. You have the hope to fulfill your destiny.

No longer will you accept people's opinions of you. No longer will you look for validation from people. God has already validated you from the foundation of the earth. He put no limits on you. YOU ARE LIMITLESS!

> Trust in the Lord, and do good; so shalt thou dwell in the land, and verily thou shalt be fed. Delight thyself also in the Lord: and he shall give thee the desires of thine heart. Commit thy way unto the Lord; trust also in him; and he shall bring it to pass. (Psalm 37:3–5)

Chapter 15

The Awesomeness of God Will Deliver You

> I shall not die, but live, and declare the works of the Lord. (Psalm 118:17)
>
> Great is our Lord, and of great power: his understanding is infinite. (Psalm 147:5)
>
> The Lord shall fight for you, and ye shall hold your peace. (Exodus 14:14)
>
> For God so loved the world, that he gave his only begotten Son, that whosoever believeth in him should not perish, but have everlasting life. (John 3:16)

The awesomeness of God will deliver you. Yes, His awesomeness has delivered you from so many things that were meant to destroy you. It doesn't matter what you are faced with right now. Know that the awesomeness of God is at work in your life. The awesomeness of God is unexplainable yet undeniable. The awesomeness of God delivers you out of the hands of your strong enemies. The awesomeness of God is working great wonders on your behalf.

The divorce that was meant to destroy you has blessed you and set you up to meet someone who will help you pursue God's visions for your life. The nervous breakdown that came to drive you out of your mind did not destroy you but stabilized you.

You can see clearer now than before. You hear God more audible than ever before. That cancer that should have taken your life didn't work against you because the awesomeness of God intercept it. He is a miracle-working God. You are alive and well to fulfill His purposes.

The job that you lost that came to take the bread off your family's table pushed you to go back to school and achieve a better-paying job. That friendship that betrayed you caused you to seek the face of God and provide you with true and sincere friends like Jonathan and King David.

And it came to pass, when he had made an end of speaking unto Saul, that the soul of Jonathan was knit with the soul of David, and Jonathan loved him as his own soul. (1 Samuel 18:1)

The people who have rejected you and thought that you would never make it, God will spread a table before you right in the presence of your enemies.

> Thou preparest a table before me in the presence of mine enemies: thou anointest my head with oil; my cup runneth over. (Psalm 23:5)

Regarding those doors that were slammed in your face, the awesomeness of God opens effectual, great doors that cannot be closed. It may be a door that you don't expect God to open or one that catapults you to the next level in your life.

> For a great door and effectual is opened unto me, and there are many adversaries. (1 Corinthians 16:9)

Regarding that sickness that came to kill you, the awesomeness of God causes you to live and not die so that you will fulfill your eternal destiny. Regarding that child who has been very disobedient in spite of how much you have been praying and fasting for change, the awesomeness of God will step in and intervene on your behalf, causing a dramatic change of heart in your child. Your child will walk in the spirit of obedience and humility. God will give your child a turning point.

Regarding the malicious and jealous family members who have come against you relentlessly, the awesomeness of God steps in on your behalf and causes peace where there was strife, joy where there were sorrows, and restoration where there was brokenness.

Regarding those Goliaths at your workplace who plague you every day even though you are doing an amazing job—they even tried to demote you—the awesomeness of God promoted you instead. He shames your enemies again.

Regarding those who hope that you will come to nothing, the awesomeness of God steps right in and catapults you to the third heaven.

> I knew a man in Christ above fourteen years ago, (whether in the body, I cannot tell; or whether out of the body, I cannot tell: God knoweth;) such an one caught up to the third heaven. (2 Corinthians 12:2)

Regarding the death of your loved one, which has brought great sorrow, hurt, and depression to you, the awesomeness of God brings divine healing and wholesomeness. When you trust that God does all things best and understand from His infinite perspective, the death of your loved ones makes more sense. The five stages of grief are accepted and adopted.

The awesomeness of God will not allow your situations and circumstances to drown you. You will not go under or be defeated because you are the head and not the tail. You are called His chosen leader and mouthpiece. You are part of His chosen generation. You are His unstoppable champion. You cannot be stopped. You will not be hindered.

God is now multiplying your heavenly inheritance. God has multiplied the things you have been praying for. It's bigger than what you expected it to be. You are His undefeated child of purpose. Even when you don't always understand what is going on, know that your heavenly partner is undefeated and is working behind the scenes of your life.

Regarding that position you applied for many times and still haven't gotten, the awesomeness of God answers yes right now. The green light is all yours. It was all about His divine timing.

Regarding the dreams that have been dormant inside you for a long time, the awesomeness of God suddenly restores them and gives you the courage to fulfill them. God has gone ahead of you. Regarding your relationship breaking up, which caused you to cry for days and nights, the awesomeness of God heals your broken heart and blesses you with like-minded people.

Regarding those traps and pits that your enemies have set up against you, the awesomeness of God gets rid of them and moves you into the palace, just as God took Joseph from the pit to the palace. You, too, will experience your palace moments. Lasting joy will ring louder in your heart. Take the limits off your life because God, your Creator, didn't put any on you. THE AWESOMENESS OF GOD IS UNDENIABLE!

Chapter 16

An Eternal Fire of Worship Has Risen in the Hearts of God's People

> And they said one to another, Did not our heart burn within us, while he talked with us by the way, and while he opened to us the scriptures? (Luke 24:32)

While praying one night, God told me that an eternal fire had risen in the hearts of God's people to worship. This eternal fire to worship was not an ordinary fire. This eternal fire to worship was not a fire that could easily be blown out. It would not be lukewarm days later. It was not the kind of fire that left people frightened or destroyed them. This eternal fire of God that has risen in the hearts of God's people is unquenchable, undeniable, and unfathomable and soaked deep into people's bones.

God revealed to me that dry bones would come to life immediately and begin to worship like never before. Our worship would be real. False worship cannot withstand this eternal fire. God's eternal fire will expose all false fires. Our worship would be fiery. The songs that would burn inside of us would deeply connect to the Holy Ghost's eternal fire. The world would see, hear, and know about this eternal fire. Why? We can't keep it silent, and we can't keep it to ourselves.

With this eternal fire, we would have an urgent and greater desire to exalt the awesome name of God. You have the right to glorify God in worship. Your worship will advance the church to a new level and into deep territories. No nations, creeds, or nationalities can deny your worship. Why? It brings true and immediate transformation to human souls.

Revival will burst forth in all nations of the earth because of the eternal fire. This eternal fire will bring in the billion-souls harvest. We will see worldwide revival displayed on social media like never before. Millions will be drawn and be transformed by the closeness of this eternal fire. Millions will not deny the power that flows out of this eternal fire. This eternal fire will set millions of altars on fire, including dead and lukewarm ones. The house of God will be a live temple of worship. Heaven will open, and divine, on-time songs will burst out of us.

Lord, let your eternal fire burn deep within your people. We need this eternal fire to take our worship into the holy of holies. We need this eternal fire to drive all the forces of hell to the lake of fire, never to return. Hell's fire is no match for this amazing eternal fire. The eternal fire will burn within our hearts and cleanse, purify, sanctify, justify, and transform us for good.

When God's eternal fire truly touches our hearts, worship will be amazing and exuberant. A blast of the Holy Ghost's eternal fire will erupt on the earth. This eternal fire will stir up the voice of God in our hearts like never before. We will hear the Spirit of truth and wisdom, telling us how to operate and to manifest this fire of worship. The world is waiting for this eternal fire to destroy devils, demons, demonic warfare, and the confusing voice of Satan and to put hell to death forever.

Come into this worship with me for the newness of life that it brings to the body, soul, mind, and spirit. Come along and see lives changed before your eyes. Come along and see the beauty of God's holiness, righteousness, unconditional love for us, twenty-four elders bowing down before His throne, and holy angels, who will worship with us. See the beauty of who God is. See the beauty of the lingering fire that rages inside of you. See the splendor of heaven, His unspeakable joy, the mystery of His glory, and His glorious power.

The eternal fire of worship will not be the usual worship. When we experience God's eternal fire, it will not be business as usual in the house of the Lord. Instead, it will be a supernatural experience, which people can't articulate with words. The Body of Christ will look different from what you are used to and what you see today. The glory of God will be manifested greater than it was with Moses at the Red Sea. God's power will be greater than when it was given to the prophet Elijah and was spoken through John the Baptist in the wilderness. God's power will be greater than what was given to the prophets and prophetesses of old.

This eternal fire will change the perception of things. Millions of people around the world will sing in tongues (heavenly languages)—even those who do not believe in speaking in tongues as the Holy Ghost gives utterance according to Acts 2:4: "And they were all filled with the Holy Ghost, and began to speak with other tongues, as the Spirit gave them utterance."

God's people will have greater excitement bursting in their hearts to attend church gladly. A new understanding and order of worship will be given. More reverence will be allocated to God. The idea of who God is will be more real to His people. Worship will be allowed to flow from free and cheerful hearts. The earthly church will now look like the early church. The upper-room experience will no longer be seen as a thing of the past. The glory, fire, and power of God will return in the universal church of Jesus Christ. The Body of Christ will have a new voice on earth!

God's people can feel the eternal fire deep within their hearts. We will not keep this eternal fire to ourselves but will spread this eternal fire to others. We will spread this good news like wildfire. We must share it with the world for them to come and experience this eternal fire that burns so fiercely in the hearts of God's people.

God's people will have more love and forgiveness for each other. God's people will have mercy and compassion for this dying world. They will give hope to the hopeless and comfort to the comfortless. We will not be able to count our relentless blessings that will make us rich and will come with no sorrows.

The pulpit will be so on fire that it will spread to the pews. This fire will spread from one person to the next. Out of this eternal fire, which is inside of the hearts of God's people, a new generation of radical worshippers will flow. It will be a new generation of God's uncompromising prophets and prophetesses who will manifest His glory and advance His holy kingdom. A new breed of spiritual counselors will break forth for such a time as this. The voices of the young will be loud and clear in this world!

The hope of God's people will become contagious. More fathers and mothers in Zion will be in the Body of Christ. A new wave of God's glory will flow out of heaven and fill the earth profoundly. New voices, which have been in hiding, will be breaths of fresh air during worship. A people with new creativity shall spring forth. A new generation of dancers will bring healing and salvation to many. Oracle singers will transform millions of lives as they worship God.

Satan will be silenced for years to come. He has no power in any of God's fire arenas. Young people will be in leadership. The Holy Ghost will divinely lead them. Males and females will be respected in the arena of worship.

> There is neither Jew nor Greek, there is neither bond nor free, there is neither male nor female: for ye are all one in Christ Jesus. (Galatians 3:28)

God's people will soar greater than the Eagles and will be catapult supernaturally to spiritual realms. The Body of Christ will hear a new sound from heaven. You will hear God's voice in a real way. Your ears will be fine-tuned to what heaven wants God's people to do in worship. New forms of deliverance will erupt. Our walk of holiness will become a lifestyle. The spirit of discernment in us will be heightened in such a way that you will be able to sniff out false worshippers and turn them into true worshippers.

> But the hour cometh, and now is, when the true worshippers shall worship the Father in spirit and in truth: for the Father seeketh such to worship him. God is a Spirit: and they that worship him must worship him in spirit and in truth. (John 4:23–24)

The eternal fire that is within our hearts will not become weary but will instead, be strengthened by the power of the Holy Ghost. The eternal fire that has risen in the hearts of God's people to worship will cause worldwide revivals. Worship will become the way God intended it to be. God's eternal fire will cause the adversary to trouble you no more.

> From henceforth let no man trouble me: for I bear in my body the marks of the Lord Jesus. (Galatians 6:17)

LET'S KEEP GOD'S ETERNAL FIRE BURNING IN OUR HEARTS FOREVER!

Chapter 17

Jesus Christ Is the Friend of All Friends

> Ointment and perfume rejoice the heart: so doth the sweetness of a man's friend by hearty counsel. (Proverbs 27:9)

> A man that hath friends must shew himself friendly: and there is a friend that sticketh closer than a brother. (Proverbs 18:24)

> Be not deceived: evil communications corrupt good manners. (1 Corinthians 15:33)

Both Christians and non-Christians can agree that Jesus Christ is the best friend and role model to have in their lives. In Jesus Christ, we can see the best qualities that human beings should aim to possess, such as genuine love, faith, courage, integrity, perseverance, generosity, faithfulness, intelligence, commitment, loyalty, and servanthood to name a few. Many scriptures teach us to become more like Jesus Christ. It is vital that we learn some of His character traits.

A true and sincere friend is one who is loving, genuine, loyal, and faithful and one who always watches out for, confides in, shares his or her life with, not jealous of you, and makes sacrifices for you. God offers us this type of amazing friendship with His precious Son, Jesus Christ. Jesus Christ is all of these things and more. Jesus laid down His life for us. That is friendship and proof that He is the greatest kind of friend we could ever have.

> Greater love hath no man than this, that a man lay down his life for his friends. (John 15:13)

If you want Him as your friend, be willing to lay down your life for Him. Jesus Christ alone died for you and me. The joy that was set before Him caused Him to endure the cross, despising the shame.

> Looking unto Jesus the author and finisher of our faith; who for the joy that was set before him endured the cross, despising the shame, and is set down at the right hand of the throne of God. (Hebrews 12:2)

It's a joy to know that Jesus Christ's death, burial, and resurrection allows you and me to be His friends forever and ever. To be a true, sincere friend to Him, we should be willing to give up our ways of doing things and start doing things God's way. Our ways of doing things lead to death. We should be willing to crucify our flesh daily.

> I am crucified with Christ: nevertheless, I live; yet not I, but Christ liveth in me: and the life which I now live in the flesh I live by the faith of the Son of God, who loved me, and gave himself for me. (Galatians 2:20)

Abraham was called the friend of God. We can become a friend of God by trusting and obeying His perfect will. Isaiah 41:8: "But thou, Israel, art my servant, Jacob whom I have chosen, the seed of Abraham my friend."

> And when he had removed him, he raised up unto them David to be their king; to whom also he gave their testimony, and said, I have found David the son of Jesse, a man after mine own heart, which shall fulfill all my will. (Acts 13:22)

Jesus Christ is the Friend of all friends. He is a friend that has been there for me from the beginning and will be at the end. In good times, He was there. In bad times, He was there. Throughout all my pain, He was there, soothing and relieving my pain. Jesus Christ is better than any painkiller or anesthetic. Indeed, Jesus Christ is a painkiller. Sometimes life hurts so much that the pain inside your heart feels unbearable. At times, I wish I could rip out the pain inside my soul. But in moments like these, I pray to Jesus and ask Him to take away the pain and He did.

You may have pain that you cannot tell anyone about except for God. Only He can understand our deepest pain because He bore all our pain on the cross of Calvary. The agony He went through while He was on the cross tells me that He understands. I am fully aware that the pain I have been through does not compare to what Jesus Christ endured for humanity. Jesus Christ paid the ultimate price for our pain.

> But he was wounded for our transgressions, he was bruised for our iniquities: the chastisement of our peace was upon him; and with his stripes we are healed. (Isaiah 53:5)

Jesus Christ is a sincere friend like no other. None can be compared to Him. He stands alone as a divine friend of all friends. We all can say we have met countless people throughout our lives, but only a few of these people have become our true friends. There are things we will go through that these friends will never understand. But Jesus Christ is touched with the feelings of our infirmities. Hebrews 4:15: "For we have not an high priest which cannot be touched with the feeling of our infirmities; but was in all points tempted like as we are, yet without sin."

Sometimes people are even afraid to share their hearts because they fear betrayal. Betrayal hurts so deep, the one who is betrayed tries harder to guard his or her heart. It's best that you don't tell people some of the things that have happened in your life. Tell them to Jesus! Sometimes when you decide to share your heart, believing and hoping that it will be kept confidential, it isn't. Tell it to Jesus!

My parents told me that some things that I went through in life should only be told to Jesus. Because every friend has a friend and that friend may not be your friend, your secret is never safe. Thanks be unto God that I have found friendship with Jesus, who is a friend like no other.

When you tell Jesus about your problems and trials, He will not be judgmental towards you. Others will judge you based on past experiences or situations. He alone can see your beginning and end. Therefore, He sees the bigger picture. He understands that trouble comes only for a season. He will not tell your secrets to others but will instead be moved with compassion towards you. He is the author and finisher of your faith. He comes through for you like no one else. Jesus Christ is the author and finisher of all friendships!

Many times, I have been betrayed by those whom I thought were my friends. I learned lessons and gained greater wisdom and new insight from each betrayal. The ability to stick closer to Jesus Christ became my number-one priority. I have come to realize more and more that developing friendship requires my investment of precious time into that person. Time is precious and must be spent wisely. God will restore the wasted years of our lives!

I have become wiser. Thanks to God for the Holy Ghost's discernment, which has helped me sniff out people immediately so that I don't waste time investing in the wrong people. When you get older, time means a lot more to you than when you were younger. Therefore, wise decisions must be made—decisions you will not live to regret later. Thank God for a divine friendship with God's only begotten Son, Jesus Christ. When all hell breaks loose against me in this life, I know, without a doubt, that I have a friend like no other to run to. Yes, I run to Jesus with all my pain, hurts, heartaches, disappointments, and sorrows.

> The words of his mouth were smoother than butter, but war was in his heart: his words were softer than oil, yet were they drawn swords. (Psalm 55:21)

> Behold, I send you forth as sheep in the midst of wolves: be ye therefore wise as serpents, and harmless as doves. (Matthew 10:16)

When the pressure of life squeezes me, I run to Jesus because He is my safe shelter, my strong and mighty tower, my deliverer, and my healer. What an awesome friend He is.

He is truly a friend like no other: faithful and true, loving, kind, gentle, and a forever, never failing friend. He loves me today and changes my tomorrows. God sees the purpose in me and fulfills it with me. He knows the depth of my brokenness. He is touched with my grief and pain and heals them. He knows the many tears I have shed and that I could not tell anyone but Him alone. How can I not love such a friend as Jesus? He is my dearest and best friend in the whole wide world. I trust Jesus Christ as my best friend wholeheartedly because He will never let me down. He will never change His love for me. He will never change His plans for my life.

From the end of the earth will I cry unto thee, when my heart is overwhelmed: lead me to the rock that is higher than I. (Psalm 61:2)

Jesus is a friend, that I trust one hundred percent, and without any hesitation or reservation. Indeed, He is my solid rock. He is awesome in all His ways. Blessed be the name of the Lord Most High. He is worthy of being praised. He is all-knowing and altogether lovely. Jesus is a perfect friend to an imperfect me.

Let me introduce you to this one-of-a-kind friend, Jesus Christ. You will never have to worry about betrayal, hurts, heartaches, or disappointments from Him as you do from people. He is a true confidant. When you tell Him what's on your heart, you never have to worry about Him telling another person. You never have to worry about His unconditional love, which remains with you at all times. Jesus Christ is the unfathomable kind of friend. Jesus Christ is a one-in-a-zillion friend. His friendship is genuine.

If He is not your friend, make Him one today. Here are some characteristics that make Jesus Christ stand out above all earthly friends: virtue, humility, prayerfulness, wisdom, faith, obedience, patience, charity, generosity, forgiveness, compassion, love, commitment, gentleness, self-control, honesty, approachability, selflessness, zeal, goodness, fairness, courage, kindness, truth, dependability, purity, holiness, responsibility, contentment, encouragement, attentiveness, enthusiasm, diligence, discretion, optimism, efficiency, appreciation, childlikeness, and the best role model to emulate. Jesus Christ possesses all the above characteristics and more.

I want to encourage everyone to get closer to Jesus Christ. You will never regret your choice. I strongly believe that the world needs a better friend and role model—Jesus Christ. Jesus Christ's positive character traits are the best ones to emulate. You can always assess your friends based on these character traits and then determine if you should invest your time before you become attached to him or her.

We can all have Jesus Christ has our real and sincere friend if we do what He commanded us to do. John 14:15 declares, "If ye love me, keep my commandments."

Jesus Christ will be your friend for all eternity. Jesus Christ is the only friend that can save your soul and give you eternal life. John 3:16 says,

> "For God so loved the world, that he gave his only begotten Son, that whosoever believeth in him should not perish, but have everlasting life."

Jesus, I am indebted to You for being my friend. You are, indeed, my friend. You are my Redeemer and Lord.

JESUS CHRIST IS A SECRET KEEPER AND A COVENANT KEEPER!

Chapter 18

Guard-Your Eyes Gate

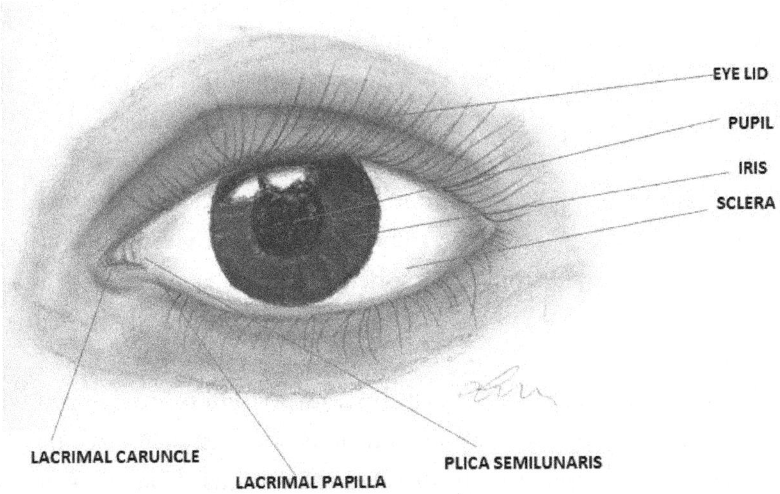

The light of the body is the eye: if therefore thine eye be single; thy whole body shall be full of light. But if thine eye be evil; thy whole body shall be full of darkness. If therefore the light that is in thee be darkness, how great is that darkness! (Matthew 6:22–23)

I made a covenant with mine eyes; why then should I think upon a maid? (Job 31:1)

> But I say unto you, That whosoever looketh on a woman to lust after her hath committed adultery with her already in his heart. (Matthew 5:28)

As you can see by the picture above, the eyes have many parts that work together to produce clear vision. Our eyes help us to see the world in all its dimensions. They help us to see people and things in various ways. Our eyes are the beauty of our souls. What we see through our eyes, we then perceive through our souls. Our eyes are extremely sensitive, and we must protect them at all times from things that can destroy them.

Human eyes come in different shapes, and beautiful colors yet have the same ability to see. Have you ever imagined what it would be like not to see? Wow, this would be very frightening for many of us. We even go to the extent of praying for our eyes daily. Many of us also pray that God will open our eyes to see the things that He desires us to see spiritually.

Help us to see Your glory, Lord. Help us to see the wonders of your heaven. Help us to see the splendor of Your throne. Help us to see the goodness of who You are and to cherish it. When we see evil things, behaviors, and actions from others, help us to be at peace and do not allow the evil that we see in this world to destroy our minds and corrupt our hearts.

We will not render evil for evil. Instead, we will overcome evil with good. For indeed, You are our good, gracious, and merciful God. It's vital that we guard our eyes gate at all times. Please guard our eyes against Satan's evil plans. Guard our eyes gate against principalities, powers, and the powers of the darkness of this world. Consecrate and free our eyes from sin, lust, and iniquities, O Lord. Keep our eyes completely focused on You, Almighty God, for only You can keep our eyes steadfast on You.

We should sever ourselves from anything that causes us to lust. We should detach ourselves from certain activities that cause us to indulge in things that pollute our eyes gate. One example would be pornography. We should separate ourselves from people who indulge in pornography so that the spirit of pornography does not influence us. We need to align ourselves with people of faith and integrity—those who are true to the Word of God and are trying their utmost to walk in God's ways.

Little eyes be careful what you see. God's eyes are infinitely greater than our finite eyes are. He can ultimately see the depth within our eyes.

Build relationships with those who will strengthen your spirit of discernment—as iron sharpens iron, so a man sharpens the countenance of his friends. Don't let your eyes see anything that will cause you to sin. Our eyes are the lights of our souls, bodies, minds, and spirits. Therefore, it is very important that we keep our eyes pure. Keeping our eyes pure and focus on God is not always easy while living in a world that is polluted by sin, shame, and disgrace. However, God's grace is enough to keep our eyes pure and focus. Purpose in your heart that you will try to keep your eyes pure. Ask the Holy Spirit to anoint your eyes with His strength to see and not give in to the pressures around you.

> For the eyes of the LORD run to and fro throughout the whole earth, to shew himself strong in the behalf of them whose heart is perfect toward him. Herein thou hast done foolishly: therefore from henceforth thou shalt have wars. (2 Chronicles 16:9)

We should use our amazing eyes to please God while serving Him wholeheartedly. Let us discern and speak the truth of God!

Holy Ghost, please expand our spiritual perception so that we will see clearer than before. We desperately desire to see greater than the Eagles. Spirit of the Living God, in the same way, that we must use binoculars by adjusting them to see objects closer, so shall You open the eyes of God's people in a new way and expand our visions.

The Holy Ghost says: "In this season the anointing is rich and will be poured out on His people's eyes, allowing us to receive new visions, dreams, and revelations. The blinders will be lifted from the eyes of His people. Scales are dropping from My people's eyes right now in Jesus' mighty name." God has great storehouses in heaven with countless treasures for His people. Once we come into His storehouse and see what He has for us. We will never be the same again. We will experience God's unstoppable praise, worship, glory, and adoration. We will never again see things the same way we use to before. Come into the deep and see the awesomeness of

God's beauty and blessings He has in store for us—unfathomable blessings that no one can stop or deny.

I ask now in Jesus's glorious name that God will open our eyes to see greater in this season. Yes, more than ever, anoint our eyes and take us to the rich kingdom that You have prepared for us who are your remnants here on earth.

God has amazing things in store for us. Hold fast. Don't give up. The pressure of life might be insurmountable but stand your ground. Stand firm, stand fast in the liberty to which you have been called. Greater days are still ahead of you. Your tomorrow will be sweeter than your yesterday. I prophesy that this is your season to receive God's best in every area of your life.

Your success is on its way. Your prosperity is on its way. God's goodness will always follow and overtake you. Your joy will return. Your sorrows will be erased. Your tears will be wiped away. Your victory is now your daily banner. Your fight is no longer yours. The champion of all battles has won it already for you. When Jesus Christ went to the cross, all your battles, troubles, burdens, sins, shame, and disgrace were nailed to the cross.

Your disappointments will bring you into greater breakthroughs. Your hope will be restored to a new level. Your eternal heavenly home is secure. All that has caused you pain will bring about your greatest miracles—miracles that can only come from God. God is a miracle worker. He works in dumbfounding ways. His miracles confound the wise. His miracles set Him apart from everyone else. His miracles will take you from the bottom of the pile and place you on the top. Yes, that's the kind of God He is—a miracle-working God. He will take you out of the pits and place you in kings' palaces. It's the season to get your life in proper alignment with God. His season is always new and fresh. It gives us a reason to live again and to have bone-deep peace that only comes through the grace of God. Newness is found in Jesus Christ. The new birth is available in Jesus Christ.

> But as it is written, Eye hath not seen, nor ear heard, neither have entered into the heart of man, the things which God hath prepared for them that love him. (1 Corinthians 2:9)

> This I say then, Walk in the Spirit, and ye shall not fulfill the lust of the flesh. For the flesh lusteth against the Spirit, and the Spirit against the flesh: and these are contrary the one to the other: so that ye cannot do the things that ye would. But if ye be led of the Spirit, ye are not under the law. (Galatians 5:16–18)

Galatians 5:16–18 encourages us to walk in the Spirit and not in the flesh. The flesh can be dangerous. When we walk in the Spirit, the desire to fulfill the lust of the flesh decrease. When we walk In the spirit, our eyes become more powerful. The more we walk in the Spirit, the less our flesh will give us trouble. The spirit and the flesh are always at war within us. Therefore, we should try our best to crucify our flesh daily and be led by the Holy Ghost.

The Holy Ghost will give us wisdom and teach us the ways we should go? It's vital in this season for us to ask God to saturate our eyes with His power, glory, goodness, and mercy.

Let's ask God to saturate our eyes with His love, compassion, joy, and victory. Let's ask God to saturate our eyes with His grace, healing, and deliverance. Let's ask God to saturate our eyes with His forgiveness, freedom, and triumphant miracles, signs, and wonders. Let's ask God to saturate our eyes with His potent Word, and with His eternal fire of glory from heaven, and a protective canopy. Let's ask God to saturate our eyes with His love, joy, peace, longsuffering, gentleness, goodness, faith, meekness, and temperance.

Let's ask God to saturate our eyes so that darkness will never overpower us so that we can run the race He has set before us as we look steadfastly upon Jesus Christ. Let's ask God to saturate our eyes with all of heaven's help and with the radiant brightness of heaven. Let's ask God to saturate our eyes so we can see His throne clearer so that His instructions will be crystal clear. If ever a time we need our eyes to be saturated, it is now. Holy Ghost saturates our eyes in Jesus' mighty name.

> The light of the body is the eye: if therefore thine eye be single, thy whole body shall be full of light. (Matthew 6:22)

> Let thine eyes look right on, and let thine eyelids look straight before thee. (Proverbs 4:25)

> The hearing ear, and the seeing eye, the Lord hath made even both of them. (Proverbs 20:12)

Jesus, please open my eyes to the works and wonders of Your hands.

Chapter 19

Lord, May You Smell the Sweet Aroma of My Praise and Worship

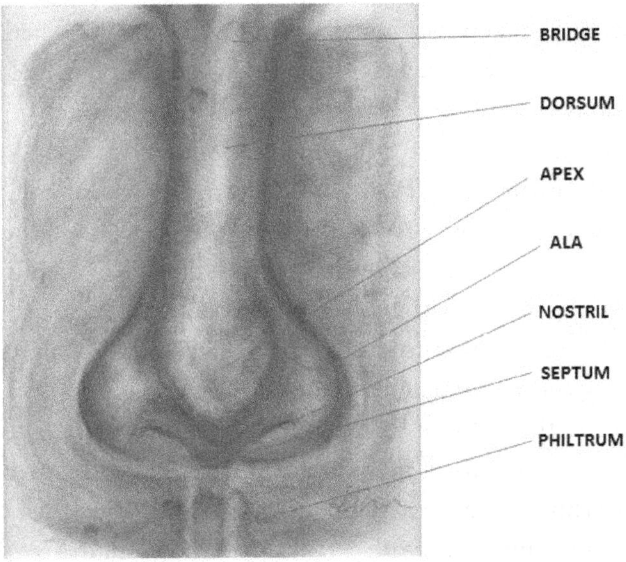

Let my prayer be set forth before thee as incense; and the lifting up of my hands as the evening sacrifice. (Psalm 141:2)

For we are unto God a sweet savour of Christ, in them that are saved, and in them that perish: (2 Corinthians 2:15)

Let the aroma of my praise and worship come into Your nostrils, Lord. My heart's desire is to fill Your nostrils with amazing, exuberant praise and worship that brings delight. Yes, my praise and worship will smell greater than the best name-brand perfumes or colognes. I desire that my praise and worship be more costly than Gold (His Sovereignty Dominion), Frankincense (His Sinless Deity), and Myrrh (His sacrificial death) that the wise men brought Jesus as a gift at his birth! LET MY PRAISE AND WORSHIP BE PLEASING IN YOUR SIGHT AND A SWEET SMELLING AROMA IN YOUR NOSTRILS!

I don't want to make noise when I praise You—because true praise is more than noise— but also want it to be intimate with God Almighty, the Creator of the Universe. I want to greet the Trinity and adore Jesus Christ, God's only begotten Son. I desire that when I praise and worship you Jehovah, I invite God into my praise and worship. Then my praise can and will reach new heights—heights beyond the veil that I have never gone to before. I want to worship you in the holy of holies!

I desire that my praise will flow into your nostrils and give sweet adoration unto the Most High God. Let the aroma of my praise and worship reach You before I even come into Your presence, in the same way, Queen Esther's scent reached the king before she did. Queen Esther filled the king's throne room with her perfume. It caused the king to become so intoxicated with her beautiful scent, and he had no choice but to extend his scepter and grant her miraculous favors. I desire that my praise and worship will be greater than Queen Esther's most expensive perfume.

Don't let the aroma of my praise and worship be forgotten, but let it have a lingering, everlasting effect on You, Lord. Psalm 100:4 declares:

"Enter into his gates with thanksgiving, and into his courts with praise: be thankful unto him, and bless his name."

Help me come boldly to Your throne with praise and worship so that my heart will be filled with Your holiness and righteousness. Let me come before You, Lord, with extraordinary and lasting praise and worship, which will always be acceptable in Your sight. Let me come boldly with my praise and worship so that I will get a clear sense of who You are and what You want me to do. Let me come boldly to Your throne with my praise and worship so that the gift of prophecy will flow out of me greater than any river. When I come boldly to your throne, You give me clear directions for my life. Obstacles are diminished in your awesome presence.

Let my praise and worship come to Your distinctive nostrils as a sweet-smelling aroma. Let it be very satisfying, Lord. Let it be pleasing, Lord. When I praise and worship You, I see things from a heavenly perspective rather than a natural perspective. Let me praise and worship You until nothing within me needs emptying. Let everything within me feel the touch of the Holy Ghost during my praise and worship unto you.

Holy Spirit, draw out your praise and worship from deep within me. Let new songs be birthed deep within me. Let new understanding, wisdom, and knowledge be granted to me.

Let me praise and worship You in a way that extinguishes pride, withholding nothing. Let me worship You as if each day was my last day on the earth. Let me praise and worship You until hell is silenced, my enemies are subdued, restoration is given to me in all areas of my life, and my chains are broken in Jesus's mighty name. Let me praise and worship You until pain vanishes and goes to the abyss of hell, and let the fire and power of the Holy Ghost flow in me so that my praise and worship will become contagious to others.

Let me praise and worship You until the house of God is full of Your glory, the church becomes like the early church, the universal church expands with the fire and power of the Holy Ghost in every service, and pastors/leaders preach and teach more on holiness, righteousness, and repentance. Let me praise and worship You until the fight of faith becomes easier, all my giants are slain, my goliaths have fallen, and Jericho walls fall flat. Let me praise and worship You until my voice becomes that of an oracle, I become the minister you have called me to be, hell is afraid of me, and borders become borderless. Let me praise and worship You until all wayward children become obedient, broken marriages are restored, and broken hearts are mended. Let me praise and worship You until peace is found more often in our present world, wars cease, nations get along, the power and glory of God fall on the earth like never before, and a new love for God is established in the hearts of billions around the world. Let me praise and worship You until You have authority in our lives, poverty is extinguished, wickedness ceases, and child molesters no longer exist. Let me praise and worship You until the reverential fear of God returns to our homes, churches, schools, workplaces, communities, and extends to the whole world.

Let me praise and worship You until the world's murder rate becomes zero, respect for parents and children returns, the lives of the innocent are no longer taken away by the wicked, the cross of Jesus Christ comes first in our world, and Bibles and prayers return to all schools. Let me praise and worship You until rape becomes a thing of the past, human trafficking stops, faith increases more than fear does, loyalty, faithfulness, and respect is restored in every marriage, our joy becomes unspeakable, and every mountain that stands before us crumbles and becomes stones for us to walk upon. Let the high praise within me begin Lord, and I will become the repairer of the breach and restorer of paths and lives.

Let me praise and worship You until addictions are subdued, and people won't drive while intoxicated but sober and save lives rather than take innocent lives; the glory of God falls like the abundance of rain, and the church gains power again in our world. Let me praise and worship You until people lead with justice and clean consciences and respect themselves and others. Let me praise and worship You until worldwide leaderships are no longer corrupt; death has no more power over us; the power of the cross is glorified; Jesus Christ's crucifixion, burial, and resurrection have full preeminence in our world; and the blood of Jesus Christ is placed on every doorpost around the world. Let me praise and worship You until those who have been placed in authority come to know Jesus Christ as their Lord and Savior and prepare themselves for His second return. Let me praise and worship You until heaven's praise and worship come to earth. Let all nations of this world speak in tongues (heavenly languages) as the Holy Ghost gives utterance; Baal worshippers turn to the True and Living Triune God and begin to worship Him in spirit and in truth; billions of souls will surrender to Jesus Christ and lift up His blood-stained banner. Let the aroma of my praise and worship come into your nostrils and dwell there forever and ever. Lord. Let my praise and worship be so deep that hell is confused and heaven rejoices.

> By him therefore let us offer the sacrifice of praise to God continually, that is, the fruit of our lips giving thanks to his name. (Hebrews 13:15)

> Let the words of my mouth, and the meditation of my heart, be acceptable in thy sight, O Lord, my strength, and my redeemer. (Psalm 19:14)

I WILL PRAISE AND WORSHIP ALMIGHTY GOD WITH ALL MY HEART, SOUL, MIND, BODY, AND SPIRIT. AMEN!

Chapter 20

Having Sweet Peace Within

God is our refuge and strength, a very present help in trouble. (Psalm 46:1)

And the peace of God, which passeth all understanding, shall keep your hearts and minds through Christ Jesus. (Philippians 4:7)

The LORD will give strength unto his people; the LORD will bless his people with peace. (Psalm 29:11)

Having sweet peace within doesn't mean my life is perfect, and everything is going well. I will admit that right now, the storms are viciously raging in my life. I have never experienced such a relentless fight from the adversary as I am now. Intense Spiritual Warfare is going on that I can't describe. My faith is tested greater than before. But I am still standing fast and firm by the grace of God!

Doubt wants to creep in subtly. Unbelief keeps knocking at my door. My destiny is in question like never before. My calling is a real struggle every day. I can't seem to find genuine human love anywhere. Betrayal is at every corner. The spirit of ungratefulness is felt deep within my heart. Loneliness sets in like dark clouds. Change looks dim on the horizon. Fear kicks in like a car after its gears have been shifted. Hope looks dim. Failure looks more certain than success. Disappointments knock me over daily. People fail me time and time again. The plans I had thought would work out did not. Shame was more easily held onto than the rope of hope and grace. A feeling of unworthiness tries to overpower me, rejection surrounds me, despair grips me daily, inadequacy sits in my mind, and depression wants to get a hold of me so badly.

In spite of all life's challenges that have tried so hard to steal my joy, I still have peace within because of Jesus Christ. I cannot explain this sweet peace to anyone. I cannot describe it in words. Joy overflows my heart like a river and drowns my problems. This joy has made me stronger in the face of my adversaries. It has motivated me to achieve, even when the odds are against me. When it seems impossible as if the walls will never come down, this peace reassures me that it is a stepping-stone or path for me to walk on freely. When problems come my way, this is how I handle them: I sing joyful songs; I encourage myself in the Lord daily, and I activate the gift of discernment and keep on going. When problems come I prophesy these words over my life: Better days are coming so I won't give up; Failure is not in my dictionary; I am victorious, and I am not a victim. It's not what it looks like in the natural, greatness runs deep within me and can only be seen in it's fullest in the supernatural realm. I won't let the spirit of fear stop God's divine destiny for me. I stay positive and remind myself that challenge is a part of my life's journey; and I reassure myself that the pain, heartbreak, hurts, betrayal and disappointments I have been through is all a set up for a miraculous comeback, for my destiny is great!

This sweet peace within my heart is so serene and beautiful. When life throws unexpected storms at me, this sweet peace has helped me to become stronger. God's peace has given me such strength and courage that I never thought I had deep down on the inside. This sweet peace within has given me a life that is worth living. I am grateful for life. I live with great expectations and joy, and as if it was my last day on earth. I have developed a great sense of humor that has helped me to combat sorrows and pain. I see the beauty in each moment. I live in the moment. I am blessed to be alive this day and forever. Thank You, Lord, for being the Giver, and Taker of life and the author and finisher of my faith.

> And said, Naked came I out of my mother's womb, and naked shall I return thither: the Lord gave, and the Lord hath taken away; blessed be the name of the Lord. (Job 1:21)

> The Lord killeth, and maketh alive: he bringeth down to the grave, and bringeth up. (1 Samuel 2:6)

No matter what life brings, I say this affirmation: "A beat-up life is better than a dead life." Life can always be restored, even when it is battered and bruised. God specializes in restoring broken lives. He does an incredible and amazing job too—a job like no other can ever do. God is not in a repairing business like auto mechanics, who keep repairing cars' parts over and over. Once God restores you, you are restored with an eternal lifetime guarantee. You are made brand-new again. You have a new beginning and can start all over again. The Holy Spirit resurrection power is now upon you for good!

You can trust God to restore your broken life. He will resurrect you beyond your wildest imagination. Give God a try today. When God is through restoring you, people will not only marvel but will also ask, "Is that really you?" They will be at a loss for words to describe your transformation. He is that kind of God. It's your restoration season. You can trust Him!

> And I will restore to you the years that the locust hath eaten, the cankerworm, and the caterpiller, and the palmerworm, my great army which I sent among you. (Joel 2:25)

You may be wondering right now how to find this sweet peace. Here are some simple steps to find sweet peace:

1. Surrender to the King of kings and Lord of lords and make Jesus Christ your personal Savior. Go to a church that preaches and teaches Bible truth and tells others about the gospel of Jesus Christ. Seek to be baptized as Jesus did.

   > Jesus answered and said unto him, Verily, verily, I say unto thee, Except a man be born again, he cannot see the kingdom of God. (John 3:3)

2. Read the Word of God daily. His Word brings perfect peace and serenity.

   > Thy word is a lamp unto my feet, and a light unto my path. (Psalm 119:105)

3. Make fasting and prayer your lifestyle.

   > And he said unto them, This kind can come forth by nothing, but by prayer and fasting. (Mark 9:29)

   > But he answered and said, It is written, Man shall not live by bread alone, but by every word that proceedeth out of the mouth of God. (Matthew 4:4)

4. Spend quality time in the presence of God daily. Have daily devotions. Get to know the Word of God extremely well. Study and meditate on it. Live it. Apply the word in all situations that you encounter.

5. Have your ears tuned into God so that you can hear what the audible voice of God and heaven are saying to you regularly? Instructions for your life are given as you stay tuned to the supernatural voice of God.

   My sheep hear my voice, and I know them, and they follow me. And I give unto them eternal life; and they shall never perish, neither shall any man pluck them out of my hand`. (John 10:27–28)

6. Be a doer of the Word. Seek to share the gospel of Jesus Christ. Be His true disciple. Win souls at any cost. Try to live a righteous life because this brings sweet peace. Be joyful, stay in the Word of God, and become mature in the things of God. Live in peace and harmony with your friends, family, and even your enemies. Some people are hard to get along with, nevertheless, try your utmost to live in peace with them. Being a disciple of Jesus Christ is a very humble process but try to enjoy the ride.

   If it be possible, as much as lieth in you, live peaceably with all men. (Romans 12:18)

   And Jesus came and spake unto them, saying, All power is given unto me in heaven and in earth. Go ye therefore, and teach all nations, baptizing them in the name of the Father, and of the Son, and of the Holy Ghost: Teaching them to observe all things whatsoever I have commanded you: and, lo, I am with you always, even unto the end of the world. Amen. (Matthew 28:18–20)

7. Plant seeds of peace and reap a harvest of righteousness according to James 3:18, which declares:

   "And the fruit of righteousness is sown in peace of them that make peace."

Pray for all leaders to possess this sweet peace within that only comes from Jesus Christ. Share your peace with others by teaching them how to obtain it. True peace can only come from the source of all sources, and that is King Jesus. He is peace all by Himself!

8. Follow God's commands, and He will allow you to walk in perfect peace. Keep putting all that you learn from the Word into practice. Keep loving the Lord daily. Those who love the Lord can have this peace. It's yours for the taking.

Let me encourage you today. No matter how hard and difficult life is, the difficulty won't last forever. The storms of life are temporary and not permanent. Take courage. This peace can be yours right now in the mighty name of Jesus. In spite of life's daily struggles, I have sweet peace within. Who could have given it to me but the Lord? Thank you, Lord! Thank you, Lord! Thank you, Lord! DON'T LET THE CARES OF LIFE DESTROY YOUR INNER PEACE!

Chapter 21

Walking the Narrow Road Is Not an Easy Journey

> Enter ye in at the strait gate: for wide is the gate, and broad is the way, that leadeth to destruction, and many there be which go in thereat. Because strait is the gate, and narrow is the way, which leadeth unto life, and few there be that find it. (Matthew 7:13–14)

> Jesus saith unto him, I am the way, the truth, and the life: no man cometh unto the Father, but by me. (John 14:6)

Walking the narrow road is not an easy journey. When you confess with your mouth that Jesus Christ is your Lord and personal Savior, He blesses you with salvation.

> That if thou shalt confess with thy mouth the Lord Jesus, and shalt believe in thine heart that God hath raised him from the dead, thou shalt be saved. (Romans 10:9)

Jesus is the way, the truth, and the life. The narrow road leads to righteousness, sanctification, holiness, purity, forgiveness, genuine love, courage, and everything that lines up with the characteristics of Jesus Christ. Walking the narrow road involves seriously making up your mind to live according to the ordinances and commandments of God. You should follow His every movement and do His perfect will willingly. Making huge sacrifices is a large part of walking the narrow road.

While we are walking the narrow road, we are going to face unexpected problems, troubles, situations, circumstances, and even detours, which often become destructive distractions in our lives. If we are not sincerely rooted and grounded in the word of God, and staying in faith through Christ Jesus, life will bring some serious issues that will cause us to stray away from the narrow road. Sometimes temptations are so strong that if we are not careful, we will fall prey to the enemy. Thank God, we have a God that will keep us from the hour of temptation. He is our faithful deliverer. He knows that humans are weak, but He is strong and mighty forever and ever.

> There hath no temptation taken you but such as is common to man: but God is faithful, who will not suffer you to be tempted above that ye are able; but will with the temptation also make a way to escape, that ye may be able to bear it. (1 Corinthians 10:13)

When we walk the narrow road, our anchor has to be well secure in Jesus Christ at all times so that giving into temptations becomes less. Yes, we are finite beings who are trying hard to walk an infinite road desperately. I am so glad that Jesus Christ walked on this earth as the Son of God and that He understands what we go through—the many trials and temptations that come upon us daily.

> And the Word was made flesh, and dwelt among us, (and we beheld his glory, the glory as of the only begotten of the Father,) full of grace and truth. (John 1:14)

Thank You, Jesus, for dying in my place on Mount Calvary. Had it not been for the cross of Jesus Christ, we would fall, time, and time again without the power of restoration. Jesus, Your cross has helped us to walk worthy of the vocation that You have called us to. Your cross has made it possible for us to continue to walk on the narrow road. Your cross has helped us understand. You, more and more. We grow in the word of God!

The way you love us with such unconditional love blows my mind. The way you forgive us is unbelievable and inconceivable. The cross of Jesus Christ gives us triple the strength, joy, and courage needed so that we can still go on joyfully even when things happen that don't make sense. Even when evil presents itself against us, and it seems as if we are losing the walk of faith, the cross gives us glorious hope. The cross of Jesus Christ grants us positive feelings instead of negative. The cross of Jesus Christ has the power to help us walk the narrow road. Staying true to your faith in Jesus Christ makes the walk bearable. When we focus on the word of God daily makes the walk a bit lighter. Fasting and prayer most definitely help us stay more focused on the narrow road.

We should always stay connected to the Holy Ghost, hear directly from the throne of grace, and respond accurately to what we hear. We should learn to apply what God gives to us. Be willing to walk in total obedience to God!

> Ye shall walk in all the ways which the Lord your God hath commanded you, that ye may live, and that it may be well with you, and that ye may prolong your days in the land which ye shall possess. (Deuteronomy 5:33)

It's important to realize that walking the narrow road doesn't exempt us from troubles and trials. However, we serve a God who will uphold us with the righteousness of His right hand. Even if we fall, He is faithful and true to forgive us and lift us up again. Walking the narrow road requires great sacrifices and self-denial. It means giving up your love for the world and follow Jesus Christ at any cost. Sometimes we will lose friends that are not going where we are going. Nevertheless, encourage them to walk on the narrow road and to receive eternal life through Jesus Christ, our Lord. We will lose family members along this narrow path because they might not be ready to come with us. However, pray for them and encourage them to come.

It's extremely important that we understand the great blessings and rewards that come from walking the narrow road. We are guaranteed eternal life, a home in paradise (heaven), to rest in God's peace forever, we don't have to worry about death anymore, no more sadness, no more sad goodbyes, no more tears, and no more pain. Evil will no longer reign. The Devil shall no longer prevail over us. In the end, it will be worth it all. It will be worth the great sacrifices we have made. We will no longer be tempted and tried. There will be no more discouragements, disappointments, or disgrace. We will no longer be slaves to sin. We will no longer feel helpless and hopeless. All this will pass, and victory will come at last!

After all our troubles and trials are over, we will sing songs of deliverance daily in the presence of Almighty God. The narrow road might be hard, but it is worth it in the end. It will come with difficulties, but once we lean on God, He will carry us through. We will overcome by the blood of the Lamb and by our precious testimonies.

> And they overcame him by the blood of the Lamb, and by the word of their testimony; and they loved not their lives unto the death. (Revelation 12:11)

I encourage you all to start walking on the narrow road. You are not walking alone. Jesus is with you every step of the way. He is holding your hand daily. Our infirmities touched him; therefore, He will comfort and cushion us even when we fall. Sometimes it may seem like the enemy is coming up against us like a flood, but remember that God is our standard against our foes. He is our victorious banner. Yes, you can expect betrayal on this narrow road but still press on. It will make sense later on. Don't give up because you are feeling broken, battered, or bruised but pour your heart out to Jesus. He will hear your cry and bring you into a place where your sorrows will turn into joy.

Trust God to do impossible things on this narrow road. Trust God to bless you tremendously beyond anything that you can ask for or imagine.

> Now unto him that is able to do exceeding abundantly above all that we ask or think, according to the power that worketh in us, (Ephesians 3:20)

Keep in mind that the sole purpose of walking on the narrow road is to gain eternal life. You are securing a place for your divine destiny.

Prayer

Dear Lord, help us to walk on Your narrow road with a spirit of humility. May we experience the great joy, blessings, peace, and abundant life and favor that comes from walking with You, Abba Father. Keep our minds focus on You, and our hearts always in tune with the Holy Spirit, in the mighty name of Jesus. Amen.

Chapter 22

The Acronym of Power and Courage

> Behold, I give unto you power to tread on serpents and scorpions, and over all the power of the enemy: and nothing shall by any means hurt you. (Luke 10:19)

> Be strong and of a good courage: for unto this people shalt thou divide for an inheritance the land, which I sware unto their fathers to give them. Only be thou strong and very courageous, that thou mayest observe to do according to all the law, which Moses my servant commanded thee: turn not from it to the right hand or to the left, that thou mayest prosper withersoever thou goest. (Joshua 1:6–7)

P is for power.

You have the power within you. Stir it up. Bring it out. Charge your power. Feed your power. Don't let your power die!

O is for the overcomer.

You are a champion in every fight of your life. You will overcome all the present situations and circumstances that you are facing. God's champion always win!

W is for worthy.

You are worthy in the presence of God. Let no one condemn you. You are God's masterpiece. You are God's precious jewel. You are God's rare diadem. You are His worthy daughters and sons. You belong to a worthy Kingdom!

E is for eternal.

You have eternal life through Jesus Christ, our Lord. John 3:16 declares, "For God so loved the world, that he gave his only begotten Son, that whosoever believeth in him should not perish, but have everlasting life."

R is for resurrection.

The cross of Jesus Christ made everything possible. You can achieve everything you set your mind to. You are the difference maker in this world. You are called Christ's world, changer. You now have resurrection life. New beginnings are now yours. Restoration is your new norm!

C is for courage.

You dare to run through the enemy's troops and to leap over walls. You dare to stand up in the face of adversaries. You dare to defeat your giants and to break down your Jericho walls through prayer.

O is for outstanding.

Your life is outstanding. You are God's outstanding warrior. Your faith is never wasted. Stand fast and live your God-given, outstanding destiny out loud.

U is for understanding.

The peace of Almighty God will grant you healing. You are gifted with wisdom and understanding. God will grant you the understanding of all situations that come into your life.

You may not understand God's timing about something, but His timing is divinely perfect.

You will be able to reveal a concealed situation!

R is for revelation.

Heaven will release its revelation deep inside you. The new revelation will come daily from the throne of grace. The new revelation will be given to you so that you can understand new situations. The true revelation of God's word will give you power over the enemy all the time!

A is for authority.

Authority is already in you. God has given you authority over all things, such as diseases, sicknesses, principalities, powers, rulers of darkness in this world, and so much more.

You are master over all your problems!

G is for guarantee.

You are guaranteed eternal life once you accept Jesus Christ as your Lord and personal Savior.

> For the wages of sin is death; but the gift of God is eternal life through Jesus Christ our Lord. (Romans 6:23)

E is for endurance.

God will give you the strength to endure your tests and trials. You will run the race of life with great endurance. You are going through situations that seem impossible to break through, but God is a situation breaker. He is your chain breaker. He is your mountain mover. He is your hell defeater. He is your stronghold destroyer. The Holy Ghost power give us endurance for life's race. You will endure to the end and win!

> And not only so, but we glory in tribulations also: knowing that tribulation worketh patience; (Romans 5:3)
>
> For ye have need of patience, that, after ye have done the will of God, ye might receive the promise. (Hebrews 10:36)

You are powerfully courageous!

Chapter 23

Let Your Life Speak for You

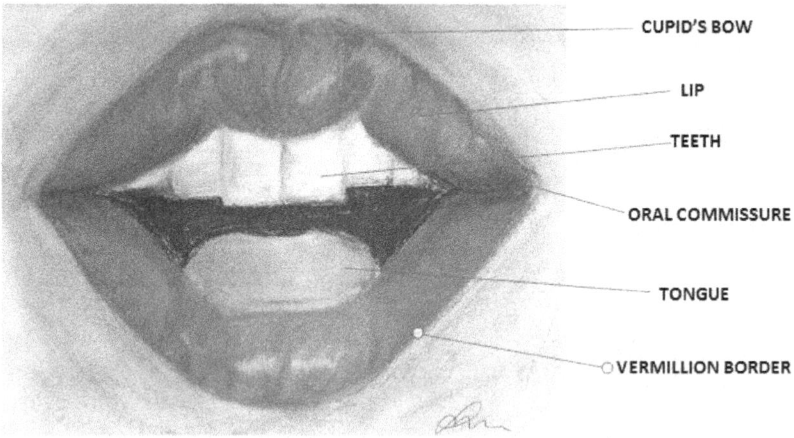

> Let no man despise thy youth; but be thou an example of the believers, in word, in conversation, in charity, in spirit, in faith, in purity. (1 Timothy 4:12)
>
> Let your speech be always with grace, seasoned with salt, that ye may know how ye ought to answer every man. (Colossians 4:6)
>
> One God and Father of all, who is above all, and through all, and in you all. (Ephesians 4:6)

Let your life speak for you. Therefore, watch your actions, thoughts, words, and conversations. It's critical to live in such a way that reflects

Jesus Christ's characteristics. A few of Jesus Christ's characteristics are obedience, blamelessness, worthiness, holiness, virtuousness, generosity, faithfulness, prayerfulness, wisdom, humility, forgiveness, stability, charity, kindness, mercy, hospitality, and gentleness.

If we want our lives to speak for us, we should make a conscious effort to emulate the characteristics of Jesus Christ. Reach out for God's grace, knowing that it's more than enough to help us to live out loud our Christian lives. God's grace is our rope of hope. Glory to God for His unmerited grace. His grace will help us endure and persevere even the cruelest pain in our lives. Let your life speak first, to your family, friends, coworkers, church members, communities, and schools and the world.

Be careful of your actions. Weigh them before you release them. Words are powerful enough to cut down someone's self-esteem and break that person's heart, over and over again. When disappointments seem impossible to overcome, trust God, and He will help you. Words have life and power, therefore use it wisely. I have seen terrible words used by great leaders to destroy great people and great nations. Encouraging words can be used to bring people together. Negative words can be used to make others feel insecure. When derogatory words are used for crushing people self-image, this can lead to revenge. Not all people know how to deal with words that are used against them in derogatory ways. But God's grace will help us forgive more easily, rather than taking revenge on others.

> Recompense to no man evil for evil. Provide things honest in the sight of all men. If it is possible, as much as lieth in you, live peaceably with all men. Dearly beloved, avenge not yourselves, but rather give place unto wrath: for it is written, Vengeance is mine; I will repay, saith the Lord. (Romans 12:17–19)

Let's use our words to give life and hope where ever we go. Let's use our words to unite and not to divide. Let's use our words to catapult people into their divine destinies. Let's treat people with love and respect. Let's encourage daily the people we come in contact with and even on social media. Let's make this world a more peaceful one by speaking positive words, one person at a time!

Let your life speak for you. Life is always on, so be careful and watch your attitudes and actions toward others. If you are a kindhearted person, don't just say that you are kind but also show kindness. If you are a loving person, show love to everyone—even the unlovable. If you are a forgiving person, start forgiving all the people who have hurt you in life and don't throw what they have done back in their faces at every given opportunity. If you are a hospitable person, accommodate others with a smile!

If you are a peaceful person, live peacefully with everyone, even though it is hard to live peacefully with some people. Some people can be very difficult. Some people even go out of their way to be mean to others and to bully others aggressively. But God's grace will bring calm to every storm.

Let your life speak by the way you carry yourself, treat people, share the gospel of Jesus Christ, perceive people in positive ways, and your demeanor. Your mannerisms show others what you believe. When people can see the fruit of the Spirit within you, they know that your life is not only bearing much fruit but that you are a living testimony of Jesus Christ to this world.

When people can see a difference in you, your life is speaking for you. When truth and righteousness make up your armor, when honesty is express in your daily life, and when your attitude is positive regardless of your obstacles, your life is speaking for you. When your joy becomes contagious, when your countenance is pleasant, and when others seek to find out about your hope in Christ Jesus, your life is speaking for you!

When you stand for justice in a world full of injustice, when God is pleased with you, and when you contend no matter what comes against you, your life is speaking for you. When you are satisfied, no matter what you have or don't have in life and have a heart of gratitude, your life is surely speaking for you. When you speak out against wrong in your society, your life is surely speaking for you. Be a voice for the voiceless!

When you can defend and be a voice for those who have none, and when you can comfort troubled souls, you are living out loud, your true conviction. When you can be a positive role model for this generation and generations to come, when your leadership promotes and doesn't demote people, and when people desire to be around you because you inspire, motivate, and elevate them to fulfill their destinies, you are living out loud!

When you are a positive influence on people, and when you are a true worshipper of God, indeed you are living out loud. You should never be ashamed of your faith and always be willing to share freely with others. When respect and love are demonstrated in your house, when you use laughter as good medicine, and when you express humor instead of despair, you are living out loud!

People won't know you because of what you say. Your actions will impact their lives. Action is doing something. We are to live the many characteristics of Jesus Christ out loud!

Chapter 24

I Am Wrapped up in Jesus Christ

> For ye are dead, and your life is hid with Christ in God. When Christ, who is our life, shall appear, then shall ye also appear with him in glory. (Colossians 3:3–4)

I am wrapped up in Jesus Christ. I have total confidence knowing that I am in God's place of protection, security, wholeness, and complete victory. I am wrapped up in Jesus Christ, where no foes can defeat me. No obstacles are big enough to overthrow the course of my destiny. No walls are so high that I cannot climb over them. If I can't climb over them, I will pray that

God will tear down these walls in Jesus mighty name. No distractions are so powerful that they will derail my God-given destiny in Christ Jesus!

Being wrapped up in Jesus Christ is a great feeling, which I cannot explain. My words fail to articulate such exuberant feelings. I know that I am in a secure hiding place with the Lord, who cares so much for me. Oh, what hope I now have and what peace I have gained. Oh, what deliverance I have received. Oh, what strength I have gained. Oh, what healing I have received. Oh, what unspeakable joy I have. Oh, what mercies are new every morning. Oh, what songs of deliverance I have deep down inside me. Oh, what laughter I have, which is better than any medicine.

I am wrapped up in Jesus Christ, and I would have it no other way. When I am wrapped up in Jesus Christ, I take His birth, death, crucifixion, burial, and resurrection seriously, and I become part of His royal kingdom. In His birth, He brought new hope to humanity, a new beginning, and a newly transformed world.

In His death, I am wrapped up in His arm of grace and protection. He serves as my spiritual blanket and covers me daily. When humanity was helpless, He became the sacrificial lamb of grace, mercy, and forgiveness. Thank God that I am hidden with Christ in God. Jesus Christ has wrapped me up in Him for His greater purpose. Eternal life is made brand-new. Eternal life is now given freely to all who will receive. I am wrapped up in Jesus Christ. Therefore, His death becomes my death, and His life becomes my life. We have the power through Jesus Christ!

Before I accepted Jesus Christ into my life, I was helpless, was sad, and had no reason to live. I was dead in my trespasses and sins and only desired to gratify my flesh. I was a sinner condemned to die, but Jesus Christ stepped in and rescued me.

Thank You for your mercy, O Lord. Thanks for Your forgiveness, O Lord. Thank you for Your loving-kindness, O Lord. Thanks for Your unconditional love, O Lord. Thanks for Your beauty for my ashes, O Lord. Thank You that at Calvary, You made things different than before.

> Now the works of the flesh are manifest, which are these; Adultery, fornication, uncleanness, lasciviousness, Idolatry, witchcraft, hatred, variance, emulations, wrath, strife, seditions, heresies, Envyings, murders, drunkenness,

> revellings, and such like: of the which I tell you before, as I have also told you in time past, that they which do such things shall not inherit the kingdom of God. (Galatians 5:19–21)

After I accepted Jesus Christ as my Lord and Saviour, I gain greater Holy Ghost anointing and power through His resurrection!

> But the fruit of the Spirit is love, joy, peace, longsuffering, gentleness, goodness, faith, Meekness, temperance: against such there is no law. And they that are Christ's have crucified the flesh with the affections and lusts. If we live in the Spirit, let us also walk in the Spirit. (Galatians 5:22–25)

I am proud to say that I have been born again in Jesus Christ. I have been baptized into Christ Jesus and His death. I have great hope of Jesus Christ glorious second coming!

> Know ye not, that so many of us as were baptized into Jesus Christ were baptized into his death? Therefore, we are buried with him by baptism into death: that like as Christ was raised up from the dead by the glory of the Father, even so we also should walk in newness of life. (Romans 6:3–4)

I am wrapped up in Jesus Christ's power and grace through His resurrection. I am now connected to Jesus Christ, the true vine!.

By His death on the cross, He took away all my sins. He suffered such cruelty as an innocent man because He refused to let me perish. Instead, He gave me eternal life. The risen Christ raised my faith higher than my expectations. My faith would have been worthless, and I would have been still living in sin if Jesus Christ had not died on the cross for me, and more importantly, He rose triumphantly from the dead on the third day!

> For if the dead rise not, then is not Christ raised: And if Christ be not raised, your faith is vain; ye are yet in your sins. (1 Corinthians 15:16–17)

> Greater love hath no man than this, that a man lay down his life for his friends. (John 15:13)

Jesus Christ's resurrection gives me a new perspective. I now set my mind on things above and not on what is happening in this world. Life is too short to focus on earthly things that will one day perish. Eternal life gives me a new and everlasting perspective and is my permanent and final destination after this life is over. Being wrapped up in Jesus Christ allows me to remember Calvary every day. I never want to forget Calvary. It is my place of hope, love, goodness, and glory. When I think of Calvary, I automatically find strength.

The resurrection of Jesus Christ is my most valuable and glorious treasure. Christ lives; therefore, I live also. I have a new life in Him, with Him, and for Him.

I am wrapped up in Jesus Christ; therefore, all my enemies are under arrest. Jesus Christ put a restraining order on all the plans of Satan. Thank You, Jesus. You are my divine deliverer! You are my hope of glory. You are my redefining beauty. You are my kind and wise heavenly Savior and friend. You are my loving Savior today, tomorrow, and to the end.

I am wrapped up in Jesus Christ. It is a feeling like no other. It's like being a newborn baby who is wrapped up by his or her mother. This baby finds a deep sense of love and security. There are no other arms that I would rather be wrapped up in than those of Jesus Christ. Falling in love with Jesus is the best love I have ever found, the greatest joy I have ever experienced, the sweetest victory I have ever tasted, and the biggest triumph I have ever encountered.

When I am wrapped up in Jesus Christ, I fear no alarm or threats from Satan, who devours. I am not afraid of the threats of Lucifer, because I know that I am an overcomer in Jesus's mighty name. My doubts are settled. My storms are calm. My tomorrow is forecasted to be brighter. My latter days will be greater. What a great, big, awesome, mighty God I serve. Thanks for Your cross, Lord. Thanks for Your death on the Cross, Lord.

Thanks for Your resurrection, Lord. Lord of lords and King of kings, I am indebted to You forever. Oh, what a marvelous wonder You are Lord. I bless Your name forever and ever!

I am wrapped up in Jesus Christ, so I don't need to fear the future. Whatever trials, sorrows, pain, disappointments, and tribulations come, God will take care of them. On the cross, Jesus took care of all the things that will come my way. He has already resurrected me spiritually. He has the keys to life, death, and hell. 1 Peter 5:7: "Casting all your care upon him; for he careth for you."

No one has greater power in this world than Jesus. No human manifestations on planet earth can compare to His splendid, miraculous, glorious and breathtaking wonders. There is no chain breaker or undefeated champion like Jesus. No one can perform signs, wonders, and miracles as He does. No one can help me overcome all my obstacles, whether they are great or small like He can and do so well. Victory is Your name, Jesus. No one can win a fight as He can. He wins all my battles and leaves my enemies dumbfounded. No one can calm the raging wind as He can. No one can shut doors that need to be shut and open doors that need to be open like He can. He is God of the impossible!

Praise the Lord. Your name is worthy of being praised. Your name, O Lord, is worthy of all exaltation. Your name is uncontestable. I am wrapped up in Jesus Christ, and there is no place I would rather be for all eternity. I am safe, secure, blessed, prosperous, successful, and unstoppable, only because of Jesus Christ.

I AM WRAPPED UP IN JESUS THE IMMUTABLE ONE!

Chapter 25

Stay in the Race

Know ye not that they which run in a race run all, but one receiveth the prize? So run, that ye may obtain. (1 Corinthians 9:24)

Life is full of ups and downs. It is full of many surprises, disappointments, hurts, and heartbreak. In spite of what comes your way in this present life, stay in the race. It won't always be easy. People will be running ahead of you. It may even seem that they are making more progress

> than you are. Just remember that God is working silently in your life and will give you the best outcome in the end.

There are days when you will feel like God has forgotten you, and you may feel discouraged but be determined and stay in the race. Victory is ahead. His banner of love is over you. Don't you dare give up, give in, or throw in the towel. He who is with you is far greater than those who are fighting against you.

Ye are of God, little children, and have overcome them: because greater is he that is in you, than he that is in the world. (1 John 4:4)

The battles you are fighting right now may seem relentless. You may feel that there is no hope in sight. Dig deep down inside, pull out your rope of hope in the name of Jesus Christ, and keep on going. Stay in the race. You will one day understand clearer why you had to go through what you went through. Things will make more sense in the end.

So be persistent and pursue your goals. Be optimistic and win the battle. Stay committed to your destiny, and someday, you will be glad that you didn't quit. Stay in the race even when quitting seems easier. Remember that quitting is not an option and it's a word that you don't use from your dictionary. Take a rest break if you must but stay in the race. You will meet many hurdles but stay in the race. Life will not always treat you fairly but stay in the race. If life knocks you down while you are in the race, get up immediately and start the race again but don't give up!

Try not to compare yourself to other people when you are running in the race.

When you compare your self with other people's process while in the race; you will take on a spirit of discouragement. Everyone is fighting their own battles, that you may not know. Stay in your lane. Stay focus and tell yourself I am in this race and I must win the prize! Remember that the greatest champion is already on your side. His name is Jesus Christ. He is a friend who never fails. Run your race with the King of kings and for the Lord of lords.

HAVE A WINNING MINDSET!

While running your race, don't cross over into someone else's lane and become automatically disqualified. Stay focused in your assigned lane. Run your best. It's never over until God seals the deal at the finish line. Try not to look back because you will become distracted, and this will take time away from your race. Stay focused and run the race that is set before you.

MIND FOCUSED-CHIN UP-EYES LOOKING AHEAD-NOW YOU ARE READY TO RUN YOUR BEST AND WIN!

Jesus is the author and finisher of your faith. Stand on the solid rock, who is Jesus Christ. He will never fail you. You are not alone in this race. He starts this race with you and will finish it with you. Keep this in your mind: Almighty God didn't bring you this far to leave you alone!

If you fall while running the race, don't stay down but get up as fast as you can and stay in the race. Keep this in mind: Falling while running isn't the end. When you make up your mind to get back up again and stay in the race, you are still in the race. It's not how you start the race that matters but how you finish it. YOU WILL FINISH YOUR RACE WELL!

Being confident of this very thing, that he which hath begun a good work in you will perform it until the day of Jesus Christ: (Philippians 1:6)

You might find yourself getting tired in the race, but it doesn't give you the right to quit. Take a mental break if you must but stay in the race. You might not get the support you thought you would expect from people. Still, stay in the race. God is your greatest fan and supporter. He will strengthen and protect you. When all hell breaks loose while you are trying to run this race, pray and take a praise break but stay in the race. Giving up is not an option.

GOD IS A WINNER AND SATAN IS A LOSER!

Therefore, my beloved brethren, be ye steadfast, unmoveable, always abounding in the work of the Lord, forasmuch as ye know that your labour is not in vain in the Lord. (1 Corinthians 15:58)

Your children might be giving you trouble. Fast, pray, and encourage them but stay in the race. Your spouse might be unfaithful to you. Seek help from a counselor and try to mend it if possible but stay in the race.

Sickness and disease come to overthrow you, stay in the race and run on with Isaiah 53:5: "But he was wounded for our transgressions, he was bruised for our iniquities: the chastisement of our peace was upon him; and with his stripes we are healed."

Read all the healing scriptures that are given in the Bible by the greatest physician-Jesus Christ, fast, pray, and seek a physician for the treatments needed but stay in the race. Your sickness and disease are only temporary and will pass sooner than you know it. The trials of your faith are only a test. Increase your faith and be healed right now in Jesus wonderful name!

Your neighbors might be acting up. Love them anyway and stay in the race. Your troubles and trials might seem unbearable, give a "happy sigh" but stay in the race, and focus on the victory that is ahead. People might speak all manner of evil against you falsely. Brush the accusations off, maintain your cool, and win the race. People might treat you unfairly. Stay in the race. Your familiar family and friends may turn against you. You are not alone. Jesus went through worse, endured the cross, despised the shame for us. Jesus Christ endured the cross to the very end even thou He went through great agony. All these things are distractions sent from hell against you so that you will drop out of the race for good.

SAY NO TO DISTRACTIONS AND YES TO STAY FOCUS AND WIN!

> For he hath made him to be sin for us, who knew no sin;
> that we might be made the righteousness of God in him.
> (2 Corinthians 5:21)

God is a man that doesn't lie. What God promised you shall surely come to pass in due season. Just be patient. He promised to be with you from beginning to the end. He will not go back on His words as humans do. He is infinite, and humans are finite. There is a big difference between the two. Trust in God's infinite power, blessings, and glory. In the end, you will never regret it. Destiny is a long-distance race that requires motivation, commitment, determination, and endurance. GOD IS TRUSTWORTHY!

Run the race with unstoppable courage, perseverance, determination, wisdom, grace, honor, and glory. Run the race, knowing that your win is not just for you alone. It is for your children, your children's children, and generations to come. By running your race well, you can speak to nations. Be a positive role model in our world. You can rise to levels beyond your wildest expectations. While you are running the race, it's very crucial to picture your victory. Prophesy to yourself using these affirmations:

> I will make it.
>
> I was born to be a winner.
>
> God created me with greatness.
>
> I was born to be God's champion.
>
> I will not be stopped.
>
> I will not be denied.
>
> I will not be hindered.
>
> The best days of my life are still ahead of me and not behind me.
>
> I am a determined eagle soaring to unfathomable heights.
>
> I am God's anointed vessel on a mission to win!

This race goes from the beginning to the end, so let's go. On your mark, get set, go, and stay in the race. SEE YOU AT THE FINISH LINE! YOU WILL BE TRIUMPHANT!

About the Author
Rev. Dr. Sanneth Brown

Rev. Dr. Sanneth Brown was born to proud parents Bishop Elijah Brown and Evangelist Estella Euphremia Brown in St. Mary, Jamaica, West Indies, as the last of fourteen children. As a Christian for twenty years, she is proud to carry the great mantle, bestowed upon her by her father, Prophet Elijah Brown, on August 10, 1994, the day before he died. God was and still is the center of the Brown family. After completing her nursing studies and training at Centennial College, Seneca College, and the University of Toronto, she became a full-time registered nurse for twenty-seven years with the PIECES Learning and Development Model of training qualifications, with a specialty in cardiac care, medical and geriatric nursing, Alzheimer's disease and Dementia.

After receiving her Bachelor of Religious education degree, being ordained as a reverend and a Certified Pastoral Counselor (CPC), she graduated with honors and received the Wesley White Award for her thesis titled "The Grace of God." She Obtained her Master of Theology degree with honors and completed her doctorate degree in systematic theology (summa cum laude). She is now an ordained minister, a Christian clinical counselor, a Christian certified marriage counselor, and an ordained chaplain.

Her passion for souls and sincere desire to see people strive to be the best that God has designed them to be, motivated her to establish a ministry called The New Testament Church of Christ the Redeemer of Canada. This is a focused prophetic church commissioned from God's Holy Throne: she speaks to nations, give clarity to those in authority, to declare and decree things yet to come, to intercede against all the plans of Satan, and to reveal the heart of a matter when it causes confusion to those in influential positions worldwide. Proverbs 29:18 says, "Where there is no vision, the people perish: but he that keepeth the law, happy is he." We must say only what God says, only what we hear from the throne of God. We believe in God the Father, God the Son, and God the Holy Ghost. This ministry is now seventeen years old. The church's mission is found in Luke 4:18–19, which says, "The Spirit of the Lord is upon me, because He hath anointed me to preach the gospel to the poor; he hath sent me to heal the broken-hearted, to preach deliverance to the captives, and recovering of sight to the blind, to set at liberty them that are bruised, to preach the acceptable year of the Lord." The church's motto is "Where thou goest I will be with thee."

Receiving awards such as, The Woman of Excellence award from the Glass Award Production, a Congratulatory letter in honor of her incredible leadership service in the community, presented by MP Shaun Chen, MP Dr. Raymond Cho, MP Rathika Sitsabaiesan, MP Neethan Shan, as well as other congratulatory letters from many members of parliament, councillors, and Canada's prime minister, Justin Trudeau, for her positive influence and tireless contributions to the community. She was also honored for her twenty years of hard work and outstanding leadership and was given an award in honor of Lincoln Alexander's legacy for Black History.

She is blessed with one son by the creator of heaven and earth, Darron Bailey Jr. He is the pride and joy of her life, her only God-blessed and prosperous child. He is spiritually ordained by the Holy Ghost to fulfill greatness in his destiny. He graduated from Ryerson University with a bachelor of psychology degree. Darron is the author of two books: his first is *Let There Be Laughs: Genesis and Exodus,* and his second is *Nine Plays for the Christians in All of Us.*

Dr. Brown enthrones Jesus Christ in her life. She reverences and honors God Almighty, her heavenly Father, and puts her entire trust in Him. Her future is secured in Christ Jesus because she is more than a conqueror through Christ that loved her (Rom. 8:37). She also believes in Matthew 28:19-20: "Go ye therefore, and teach all nations, baptizing them in the name of the Father, and of the Son, and of the Holy Ghost: Teaching them to observe all things whatsoever I have commanded you:

and, lo, I am with you always, even unto the end of the world. Amen." She believes in Ephesians 6:19–20: "And for me, that utterance may be given unto me, that I may open my mouth boldly, to make known the mystery of the gospel, for which I am an ambassador in bonds: that therein I may speak boldly, as I ought to speak." Writing this book is yet another piece to add to her divinely orchestrated achievements.

OTHER BOOKS WRITTEN BY THE AUTHOR

NOW IS THE TIME FOR DISCERNMENT

THE HOLY SPIRIT PROPHETIC POETIC JOURNAL

THE HOLY SPIRIT PROPHETIC POETIC PRAYERS

CPSIA information can be obtained
at www.ICGtesting.com
Printed in the USA
LVHW081203160719
624251LV00002B/2/P